Grammar and punctuation

Teacher's Resource Book

Author
Huw Thomas and Graham Fletcher

Editorial Team
Rachel Morgan, Melissa Somers,
Jenny Wilcox, Marion Archer
and Red Door Media Ltd

Series designers
Shelley Best and Anna Oliwa

Design team
Nicolle Thomas and Neil Salt

Illustrations
Moreno Chiacchiera/Beehive Illustration

**CD-ROM design and
development team**
Hannah Barnett, Phil Crothers
and MWA Technologies Private Ltd

Designed using Adobe Indesign
Published by Scholastic Ltd,
Book End, Range Road, Witney,
Oxfordshire OX29 0YD
www.scholastic.co.uk

Printed by Ashford Colour Press
© 2015 Scholastic Ltd
1 2 3 4 5 6 7 8 9 0 5 6 7 8 9 0 1 2 3 4

British Library Cataloguing-in-Publication Data
A catalogue record for this book is available from
the British Library.
ISBN 978-1407-14069-8

Acknowledgements

Every effort has been made to trace copyright holders for the works reproduced in this book, and the publishers apologise for any inadvertent omissions.

Extracts from *The National Curriculum in English, English Programme of Study* © Crown Copyright. Reproduced under the terms of the Open Government Licence (OGL). http://www.nationalarchives.gov.uk/doc/open-government-licence/open-government-licence.htm

Contents

Chapter 1
Verbs and tenses

Chapter 2
Formal and informal speech and writing

Chapter 3
Complexities in sentences

Chapter 4
Cohesion, organisation and presentation

Chapter 5
Punctuation

Chapter 6
Getting to grips with grammar

Introduction

Scholastic English Skills: Grammar and punctuation

This series is based on the premise that grammar and punctuation can be interesting and dynamic – but on one condition. The condition is that the teaching of these grammar aspects must be related to real texts and practical activities that experiment with language, investigate the use of language in realistic contexts and find the ways in which grammar and punctuation are used in our day-to-day speech, writing and reading. This book encourages children to look back at their written work and find ways to revise and improve it.

Teaching grammar and punctuation

'As a writer I know that I must select studiously the nouns, pronouns, verbs, adverbs, etcetera, and by a careful syntactical arrangement make readers laugh, reflect or riot.'

Maya Angelou

The *Scholastic English Skills: Grammar and punctuation* series equips teachers with resources and subject training to enable them to teach grammar and punctuation effectively. The focus of the resource is on what is sometimes termed 'sentence-level work', so called because grammar and punctuation primarily involve the construction and understanding of sentences.

Many teachers bring with them a lot of past memories when they approach the teaching of grammar. Some will remember school grammar lessons as the driest of subjects, involving drills and parsing, and will wonder how they can make it exciting for their own class. At the other end of the spectrum, some will have received relatively little formal teaching of grammar at school. In other words, there are teachers who, when asked to teach clause structure or prepositions, feel at a bit of a loss. They are being asked expectantly to teach things they are not confident with themselves.

Grammar can evoke lethargy, fear, irritation, pedantry and despondency. Yet as demonstrated by the above comment from Maya Angelou, even one of our greatest modern writers presents her crafting of sentences as an exciting and tactical process that has a powerful effect on her readers. Can this be the grammar that makes teachers squirm or run?

About the product

The book is divided into six chapters. Each chapter looks at a different aspect of grammar and punctuation and is divided into sections. Each section includes teachers' notes – objective, background knowledge, notes on how to use the photocopiable pages, further ideas and digital content – and up to three photocopiable pages.

Posters

Each chapter has two posters. These posters are related to the contents of the chapter and should be displayed and used for reference throughout the work on the chapter. The poster notes (on the chapter introduction page) offer suggestions for how they could be used. There are black and white versions in the book and full-colour versions on the CD-ROM for you to print out or display on your whiteboard.

Activities

Each section contains three activities. These activities all take the form of a photocopiable page which is in the book. Each photocopiable page is also included on the CD-ROM for you to display or print out (answers are also provided, where appropriate, in a separate document on the CD-ROM).

Many of the photocopiable pages have linked interactive activities on the CD-ROM. These interactive activities are designed to act as starter activities to the lesson, giving whole-class support on the information being taught. However, they can also work equally well as plenary activities, reviewing the work the children have just completed.

Workbooks

Accompanying this series is a set of workbooks containing practice activities which are divided into chapters to match the teacher's resource book. Use a combination of the photocopiable pages in this book and the activities in the workbook to help children practise and consolidate grammar and punctuation skills.

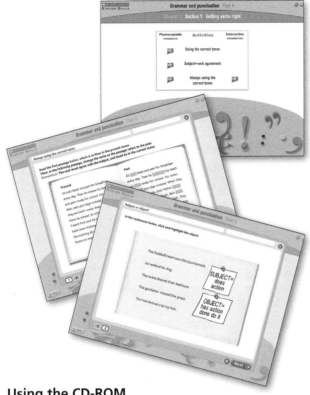

Using the CD-ROM

Below are brief guidance notes for using the CD-ROM. For more detailed information, see 'How to use this Digital content' on the Main menu.

The CD-ROM follows the structure of the book and contains:

- All of the photocopiable pages.
- All of the poster pages in full colour.
- Answers provided, where relevant.
- Interactive on-screen activities linked to the photocopiable pages.

Getting started

Put the CD-ROM into your CD-ROM drive.

- For Windows users, the install wizard should autorun, if it fails to do so then navigate to your CD-ROM drive. Then follow the installation process.
- For Mac users, copy the disk image file to your hard drive. After it has finished copying double click it to mount the disk image. Navigate to the mounted disk image and run the installer. After installation the disk image can be unmounted and the DMG can be deleted from the hard drive.
- To install on a network, please see the ReadMe file located on the CD-ROM (navigate to your drive).

To complete the installation of the program you need to open the program and click 'Update' in the pop-up. Please note – this CD-ROM is web-enabled and the content will be downloaded from the internet to your hard-drive to populate the CD-ROM with the relevant resources. This only needs to be done on first use, after this you will be able to use the CD-ROM without an internet connection. If at any point any content is updated you will receive another pop-up upon start up with an internet connection.

Main menu

The main menu is the first screen that appears. Here you can access: terms and conditions, registration links, how to use the CD-ROM and credits. To access a specific year group click on the relevant button (NB only titles installed will be available). To browse all installed content click **All resources**.

Chapter menu

The Chapter menu provides links to all of the chapters or all of the resources for a specific year group. Clicking on the relevant Chapter icon will take you to the section screen where you can access the posters and the chapter's sections. Clicking on **All resources** will take you to a list of all the resources, where you can search by keyword or chapter for a specific resource.

Section menu

Here you can choose the relevant section to take you to its activity screen. You can also access the posters here.

Activity menu

Upon choosing a section from the section menu, you are taken to a list of resources for that section. Here you can access all of the photocopiable pages related to that section as well as the linked interactive activities.

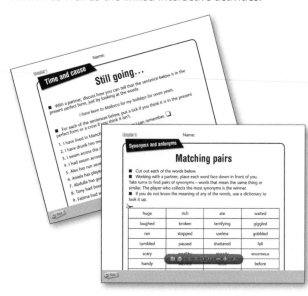

All resources

All resources lists all of the resources for a year group (if accessed via a Chapter menu) or all of the installed resources (if accessed via the Main menu). You can:

- Select a chapter and/or section by selecting the appropriate title from the drop-down menus.
- Search for key words by typing them into the search box.
- Scroll up or down the list of resources to locate the required resource.
- To launch a resource, simply click on the **Go** button.

Navigation

The resources (poster pages, photocopiable pages and interactive activities) all open in separate windows on top of the menu screen. To close a resource, click on the **x** in the top right-hand corner of the screen and this will return you to the menu screen.

Closing a resource will not close the program. However, if you are in a menu screen, then clicking on the **x** will close the program. To return to a previous menu screen, you need to click on the **Back** button.

Teacher settings

In the top left-hand corner of the Main menu screen is a small **T** icon. This is the teacher settings area. It is password protected, the password is: login. This area will allow you to choose the print quality settings for interactive activities 'Default' or 'Best'. It will also allow you to check for updates to the program or re-download all content to the disk via **Refresh all content**.

Answers

The answers to the photocopiable pages can be found on the CD-ROM in the All resources menu. The answers are supplied in one document in a table-format, referencing the page number, title and answer for each relevant page. The pages that have answers are referenced in the 'Digital content' boxes on the teachers' notes pages. Unfortunately, due to the nature of English, not all pages can have answers provided because some activities require the children's own imaginative input or consist of a wider writing task.

Objectives

Objectives

Page	Section	English skills objective	To use commas to clarify meaning or avoid ambiguity in writing.	To use hyphens to avoid ambiguity.	To use brackets, dashes or commas to indicate parenthesis.	To use semicolons, colons or dashes to mark boundaries between independent clauses.	To use a colon to introduce a list and semicolons within a list.	To punctuate bullet points correctly.	To know how words are related by meaning as synonyms or antonyms.	To link ideas across paragraphs using a wider range of cohesive devices: repetition of a word or phrase, grammatical connections and ellipsis.	To use layout devices.
81	Linking ideas across paragraphs	Link ideas across paragraphs using cohesive devices.								✓	
85	Writing cohesively	Use a wide range of cohesive devices effectively.								✓	
89	Presenting writing	Use organisational and presentational devices to structure text.						✓			✓
93	Guiding the reader	Use layout devices to structure text and guide the reader.						✓			✓
97	Organising writing	Write cohesively, considering how to organise and present writing.							✓	✓	✓
104	Colons, semicolons and dashes	Use a colon to introduce a list and semicolons within lists.					✓				
108	Separating clauses	Use colons, semicolons and dashes to mark the boundary between independent clauses.				✓					
112	Hyphens	Understand how hyphens can be used.		✓							
116	Using punctuation	Apply knowledge of punctuation.	✓	✓	✓	✓	✓				
120	Punctuation in writing	Secure the use of a wide range of punctuation in writing.	✓	✓	✓	✓	✓				
127	Revision of word classes	Revisit different words classes and consider their functions in sentences.									
131	More on word classes	Revisit different words classes and consider their functions in sentences.									
135	Sentences	Identify sentences with different forms and learn to use them in writing.									
139	Combining words, phrases and clauses	Use different kinds of clause in writing and combine words, phrases and clauses using a variety of conjunctions.									
143	Words at work	Experiment with word classes, clauses and conjunctions to improve sentence writing.									

Chapter 4 — rows 81–97
Chapter 5 — rows 104–120
Chapter 6 — rows 127–143: Chapter 6 revises and consolidates grammar work that the children will have covered during Key Stage 2.

Chapter 1

Verbs and tenses

Introduction

This chapter is devoted to understanding the use of verbs. Children will identify different types of verbs through a variety of activities. They will explore how verbs can mark time/cause and recap the work done on subject–verb agreement in Year 5. They then look at the use of modal verbs and build on the knowledge they have gained in Year 5. The final activities develop the children's understanding of the perfect form and their use of adverbs. Some activities ask the children to identify the different tenses, but the focus is mostly on the functions of verbs in particular contexts. For further practice, please see the 'Verbs and tenses' section of the Year 6 workbook.

In this chapter

Getting verbs right page 12	Ensure subject–verb agreement and correct and consistent use of tense in writing.
Time and cause page 16	Understand how verbs can mark relationships of time and cause.
Showing time and cause using verbs page 20	Use the perfect form of verbs to mark relationships of time and cause.
Modal verbs and adverbs page 24	Indicate degrees of possibility using modal verbs and adverbs.
Writing with verbs page 28	Use verb forms and verb tenses correctly and consistently in writing and use verbs and adverbs to indicate degrees of possibility.

Poster notes

Using verbs to show time and cause (page 10)
This poster displays the ways verbs show the timing of events through the use of different tenses. It also shows how the same sentences can have causes attributed to them to provide further explanation for the reader. Invite children to use this format to devise their own sentences including time/cause.

Modal verbs (page 11)
This poster shows the relative degree of possibility of different modal verbs. Display it in the classroom and explain to the children that these verbs are always added to other verbs. Remind them that these verbs can be made negative by the addition of 'not', for example: *I will not finish reading this book tonight*.

Vocabulary

Children should already know:
verb, modal verb, adverb, tense (past, present)
In Year 6 children need to know:
subject, object

Verbs and tenses

Using verbs to show time and cause

A verb is a word that tells us that an action or an event is taking place.

Time tells us when something happens.

This happened in the past.

This is happening now.

This will happen in the future.

Ranvia worked hard for her examinations.

Ranvia is taking her examinations.

Ranvia will get the results of her examinations.

These are the causes of the actions.

Ranvia worked hard for her examinations so she would be confident of passing them.

Ranvia is taking her examinations because she wants to go and do well in them.

Ranvia will get the results of her examinations because they have now been marked.

SCHOLASTIC
www.scholastic.co.uk

Verbs and tenses

MODAL VERBS

**Modal verbs express possibility, probability, permission and obligation.
Do you know which modal verbs show the most and least likely outcomes?**

Degree of possibility	Modal verb	Example
certainty	will	I **will** finish reading this book tonight.
	can	We **can** win this match.
	shall	I **shall** go out tonight.
probable	must	I **must** take the penalty.
	should/ought	I **should/ought** to do my homework.
	would	I **would** extend the school holidays, if I were the prime minister.
possible	might	I **might** score a goal.
	may	I **may** have jelly for tea.
	could	I **could** clean my room.

Getting verbs right

Objective

Ensure subject–verb agreement and correct and consistent use of tense in writing.

Background knowledge

Children should be aware of the need to use the correct subject–verb agreement when using singular and plural verbs. Introduce the children to the term 'subject', which is the person or thing that performs the action that the verb indicates. For example, in *John ran*, 'John' is the subject and 'ran' is the verb. Subject–verb agreement takes place when the correct subject is coupled with the correct form of the verb. So *John ran* is correct, *John and Joan ran* is correct, *John and Joan run* is correct, and *John runs* is correct; but *John and Joan runs* is incorrect.

Activities

● **Photocopiable page 13 'Subject–verb agreement'**
This sheet gives children combinations of subjects and verbs and asks them to explain why one combination is incorrect (does not have subject–verb agreement). Ask the children to fill in the boxes with the correct answers to describe the pictures. There are always two correct answers for each picture. Finally, invite the children to discuss with a partner why there is more than one correct answer. They should conclude that it is because the subject matches different forms of the verb in each example. For example: *John walks* is correct in the present form, but *Evan walked* is correct in the past form.

● **Photocopiable page 14 'Using the correct tense'**
Remind children of the need to use the correct tense and for subject–verb agreement by asking them to put appropriate verbs into the sentences on the sheet. There

will be many possible answers but the form of the verb will be determined by the clues in the sentence. For example, sentence 1 starts with 'Yesterday' so the verb form must be the past tense. It must also be singular because the subject is 'I'. Challenge the children to show their understanding of what they have done by explaining two of their choices.

● **Photocopiable page 15 'Always using the correct tense'**
The sheet provides the children with a sample text set in the present. Ask the children to transpose verbs from the present to the past and future time. This will also help remind them of the need for subject–verb agreement. The sheet includes a mix of verbs with some that take 'ed' in the past tense and those that do not.

Further ideas

● **Subject–verb matching:** Make a set of three subject flash cards with two names on one and a single name on the other two. Make a second set of verb flash cards with different forms of the verbs 'to go', 'to have', 'to play', 'to do', 'to walk', and 'to run'. Ask the children to shuffle both sets and deal one from each. Can they decide if the subject and the verb agree?

● **Being consistent:** Invite the children to write their own story of a day in the present tense. Ask them to swap their stories with a partner and then transpose their partner's work into the past tense. They should then swap back and assess each other's work.

Digital content

On the digital component you will find:
● Printable versions of all three photocopiable pages.
● Answers for all three photocopiable pages.
● Interactive version of 'Always using the correct tense'.

Getting verbs right

Subject–verb agreement

Subject–verb agreement takes place when the subject is coupled with the correct form of the verb. For example: *Evan ran* is correct, but *Evan and Maya runs* is not.

■ Explain why *Evan and Maya runs* is not correct.

_____

_____

_____

■ Look at the pictures below. Choose the statements with the correct subject–verb agreement and write them in the last column. There will always be more than one correct answer. The first one has been done for you.

1.	Evan walk. Evan walks. Evan walked.	Evan walks. Evan walked.
2.	Evan and Maya eat. Evan and Maya ate. Evan and Maya eats. Evan and Maya eaten.	
3.	Evan swim. Evan swam. Evan swims.	
4.	Evan jumps. Evan jumped. Evan jump.	

■ Discuss with a partner why there is more than one correct answer for each picture and write your answer below.

_____

_____

_____

Name:

Getting verbs right

Using the correct tense

■ Use the clues in the sentences below to help you choose appropriate verbs to fit the gaps.

Hint! There are many possible answers but remember that the verb must **agree with the subject**, and must be in the **correct tense**.

1. Yesterday I _____ a film.

2. We _____ on holiday next week.

3. The school _____ everyday.

4. I _____ my homework now.

5. Laura _____ shopping after school.

6. We _____ a new English teacher in September.

7. August _____ always hot in Greece.

8. I _____ my homework in the car on the way to school.

9. This morning I _____ football with Marius and Gomez.

10. The holidays _____ a long time ago.

■ Pick two of your sentences and explain which form of the verb you have used and why you think it is correct.

Sentence number: _____
I used the past / present / future form of the verb because

_____

_____

Sentence number: _____
I used the past / present / future form of the verb because

_____

_____

PHOTOCOPIABLE   ■SCHOLASTIC
www.scholastic.co.uk

Getting verbs right

Always using the correct tense

■   Read the passage below, which is written in the present tense. Then in the following two passages change the verbs to ensure the passages are in either the past or future time.

Present

Ali eats toast and jam for breakfast every day. Then he cleans his teeth and gets ready for school. His sister, Bela, eats porridge instead. When they are both ready, their father takes them to school. At school, Bela has French first and Ali has English. They both learn history in the afternoon. In the evening Ali watches TV and Bela listens to music.

Remember! The verb must **agree with the subject**, and must be **in the correct tense**.

Past

Ali _____ toast and jam for breakfast every day.

Then he _____ his teeth and _____

ready for school. His sister, Bela, _____ porridge

instead. When they _____ both ready, their

father _____ them to school. At school, Bela

_____ French first and Ali _____

English. They both _____ history in the

afternoon. In the evening Ali _____ TV and Bela

_____ to music.

Future

Ali _____ toast and jam for breakfast every day.

Then he _____ his teeth and _____

ready for school. His sister, Bela, _____ porridge

instead. When they _____ both ready, their

father _____ them to school. At school, Bela

_____ French first and Ali _____

English. They both _____ history in the

afternoon. In the evening Ali _____ TV and Bela

_____ to music.

Time and cause

Objective

Understand how verbs can mark relationships of time and cause.

Background knowledge

Children need to understand what the perfect form means and use it to explain relationships of time and cause. It's important to remember that the past perfect and the present perfect both refer to the **past**. The key to knowing which form to use is in knowing how far in the past the events occurred.

If it has happened and is completed, we use the **past perfect** form, using 'had' with the past participle of another verb (the part that usually ends in 'ed' – though some verbs, such as 'to be', have irregular past participles). For example: *Shirley had walked home*. In this sentence, Shirley is no longer there so the action has been completed.

If the action has happened but is still continuing, we use the **present perfect** form, using 'have' or 'has' with the past participle of another verb. For example: *Shirley has walked home all week*. In this sentence the action started a week ago and is continuing today. To create the **present perfect continuous**, we use 'have' or 'has' with the present participle (the part of the verb that ends in 'ing'). For example: *Shirley has been walking home all week*.

Activities

● **Photocopiable page 17 'It's in the past'**
This sheet helps the children identify the past perfect form and challenges them to explain how to recognise it. Children should recognise that the example sentence includes 'had' and 'walked' together, showing that the action has been completed, so is in the past perfect form. The correct past perfect form sentences are: 2, 4, 5, 7, 9 and 10.

● **Photocopiable page 18 'Still going…'**
This sheet focuses on the present perfect form and asks children to explain how to recognise it. Children should recognise that the use of *have been* and *for seven years* suggests the action has been going on for a long time and is still continuing, so is in the present perfect form. The correct present perfect form sentences are: 1, 2, 5, 6, 7 and 10.

● **Photocopiable page 19 'Is it over?'**
This sheet tests the children's understanding of the work they have done on the past perfect and the present perfect. The children are given a range of sentences and asked to rewrite them either in the past perfect or the present perfect form. Finally, they are asked to make up two of their own sentences in each form.

Further ideas

● **Examples:** Provide the children with reading materials in which they can find examples of the past perfect and present perfect forms.
● **Examining examples:** When children find examples, ask them to explain how they know that they are past perfect or present perfect forms.

Digital content

On the digital component you will find:
● Printable versions of all three photocopiable pages.
● Answers for all three photocopiable pages.
● Interactive version of 'It's in the past' and 'Still going…'.

Time and cause

It's in the past

■   With a partner, discuss how you can tell that the sentence below is in the past perfect form, just by looking at the words.

Shirley had walked home.

■   For each of the sentences below, put a tick if you think it is in the past perfect form or a cross if you think it isn't.

1. I had pizza for tea. ☐
2. I had eaten chips for tea. ☐
3. I jumped across the stream. ☐
4. I had jumped across the stream. ☐
5. I had been to Mallorca. ☐
6. Lizzie has been to America. ☐
7. Amy had bought an MP3 player. ☐
8. Farzal went outside. ☐
9. Manjula had listened to the instructions. ☐
10. Eli had completed his work. ☐

■   Pick two of your answers. Explain why you think one is in the past perfect form and one is not.

Sentence number: _____ IS in the past perfect form because

_____

_____

Sentence number: _____ IS NOT in the past perfect form because

_____

_____

Name:

Time and cause

Still going...

■ With a partner, discuss how you can tell that the sentence below is in the present perfect form, just by looking at the words.

I have been to Mallorca for my holidays for seven years.

■ For each of the sentences below, put a tick if you think it is in the present perfect form or a cross if you think it isn't.

1. I have lived in Manchester for as long as I can remember. ☐
2. I have drunk too much lemonade. ☐
3. I swam across the river. ☐
4. I had swum across the river. ☐
5. Alex has run several marathons. ☐
6. Aniela has played the piano since she was young. ☐
7. Abdulla has gone to Australia. ☐
8. Tony had bought a new car. ☐
9. Fatima had seen the evening stars. ☐
10. Ben has started his new job. ☐

■ Pick two of your answers. Explain why you think one is in the present perfect form and one is not.

Sentence number: _____ IS in the present perfect form because

_____

_____

Sentence number: _____ IS NOT in the present perfect form because

_____

_____

PHOTOCOPIABLE ■SCHOLASTIC
www.scholastic.co.uk

Time and cause

Is it over?

When we talk about an action from the past that has finished, we use the past perfect form. When we talk about an action from the past that is still happening, we use the present perfect form.

■ The following sentences are all written in the simple present form. Rewrite them so that they are in the past perfect form.

1. I study English at school.

_____

2. Barnes plays video games.

_____

3. Alexis cooks breakfast.

_____

■ The following sentences are all written in the simple present form. Rewrite them so that they are in the present perfect form.

4. I read novels in English at school.

_____

5. Alice plays ten-pin bowling.

_____

6. Margaret swims every day.

_____

■ Now make up two sentences of your own. One must be in the past perfect form and the other in the present perfect form.

_____

_____

Showing time and cause using verbs

Objective

Use the perfect form of verbs to mark relationships of time and cause.

Background knowledge

This section is a continuation of the last one. Remind the children that they need to be able to recognise the past perfect and present perfect forms of verbs. Both forms refer to the past. They need to be able to differentiate between them and their uses. If it has happened and is completed, we use the past perfect form. If it has happened but is still continuing, we use the present perfect form. The children need to know that 'have' and 'has' are used with the past participle of another verb to create the present perfect form. The past perfect form is created by using 'had' with the past participle of another verb. The activities in this section enable the children to make further progress in their ability to both forms of verbs in extended pieces of writing.

Activities

● **Photocopiable page 21 'A postcard home'**
This is a short activity to test the children's understanding of the present perfect form. Ask them to write a postcard, explaining what they have been doing continually, throughout the week. They can write from their own experience or make it up.

● **Photocopiable page 22 'Dear diary'**
This diary-writing activity requires children to write in the past perfect form. They are given a timetable for their first day at secondary school. Invite children to write a diary entry as if it is at the end of their first day. They do not need to write about all aspects of the day listed.

● **Photocopiable page 23 'Put it back!'**
This final activity on the present perfect and past perfect forms revises the work the children have done so far. The first activity tests their ability to recognise the forms. The second asks them to adapt sentences into the two forms. The final activity asks them to make up their own sentences using the different forms. Correct answers for the first activity are: present perfect – 1 and 3; past perfect – 2 and 4.

Further ideas

● **'I have…' board:** Write *I have…* at the top of an A1 piece of paper and ask the children to write sentences underneath about what they have done this week. This could be done at times when they have finished activities early. Ask the children to see if there are any unique 'I have…' statements on the board. Encourage them to check that all the statements are actually in the present perfect form and are not statements like *I have a dog*.

● **By the time I was:** Ask the children: *Can you think of something you had done by the age of eight?* They should reply using the past perfect form, for example: *By the time I was eight I had learned to swim*. Follow this with similar questions using different ages for different children.

Digital content

On the digital component you will find:
● Printable versions of all three photocopiable pages.
● Answers to 'Put it back!'.

Showing time and cause using verbs

A postcard home

■ Imagine you are on holiday and are sending this postcard to one of your friends. Use the present perfect form to write about what you have done while you have been away and why you have done it.

Remember to keep your sentences short and just outline the main events.
For example:

The weather has been glorious all week. I have been in the sea every day because it has been so hot.

Dear

_____

_____

_____   _____

_____   _____

_____   _____

_____   _____

SCHOLASTIC
www.scholastic.co.uk   **PHOTOCOPIABLE**   **Scholastic English Skills**
Grammar and punctuation: Year 6   **21**

Name:

Showing time and cause using verbs

Dear diary

■ Imagine you have just started secondary school. Read the notes below, listing the timetable for your first day.

8.45–9.00	9.00–10.00	10.00–11.00	11.00–11.15	11.15–12.15
Year 7 talk by the head teacher (school hall)	Period 1: Form period with your form tutor	Period 2: History	Break (Year 7 yard) Prefects will be available to help you find your rooms for Period 3	Period 3: Mathematics
12.15–1.00	**1.00–1.10**	**1.10–2.10**	**2.10–3.10**	
Lunch	Form period	Period 4: French	Period 5: Science	

■ Write a diary entry about your first day at school. Use the past perfect form and the timetable above to describe what you did on your first day.

2 September

Dear Diary

_____

_____

_____

_____

_____

Showing time and cause using verbs

Put it back!

■ Decide whether each sentence below is in the past perfect or the present perfect form. Write it on the line.

1. I have done some of my homework. _____

2. My brother had missed the bus. _____

3. My nan has lived in the same house all of her life. _____

4. Nadia had become a successful runner. _____

■ Rewrite the following sentences using the form shown in brackets.

5. The football team is playing in the Cup Final. **(Past perfect)**

_____

6. I am eating curry for tea. **(Past perfect)**

_____

7. I am going to the park. **(Present perfect)**

_____

8. Sadie enjoys watching TV. **(Present perfect)**

_____

■ Write your own sentences below, using the past perfect and present perfect forms. Explain how you know each are in that form.

Past perfect: _____
I know this is in the past perfect form because

_____

_____

Present perfect: _____
I know this is in the present perfect form because

_____

_____

Modal verbs and adverbs

Indicate degrees of possibility using modal verbs and adverbs.

Background knowledge

Modal verbs never function on their own as main verbs – they are auxiliary verbs used to indicate the conditions or likelihood of a main verb. For example, *I eat food* is a statement indicating the strong likelihood of an action. Whereas *I might eat food* implies it is less likely.

There are three main forms of modal verb, each with different grades of strength. Opinion and context may change their degree of strength, but examples are shown below. The strongest modal verb is at the top and the weakest is at the bottom.

	Certainty	Ability	Obligation
Strongest	will	can	must
Weakest	shall would might may	could	should ought

Adverbs can also be used to modify verbs to show degrees of possibility. Many end in 'ly' so are easily recognisable, such as 'rarely'. Other adverbs of certainty are less easy to recognise, such as 'always', 'only', 'never', 'ever', 'still', 'just', 'perhaps' and 'surely'.

Activities

● **Photocopiable page 25 'How likely is it?'**
This activity builds on the work the children have done on modal verbs in Year 5. The children are given a grid showing examples of the degree of possibility related to different modal verbs. Ask them to use this to insert an appropriate modal verb into a range of sentences. There could be more than one possible answer for each sentence, so it is up to the children to decide upon the degree of possibility. In the example, it is very unlikely that the tiger would come to tea, but as Judith Kerr's story *The Tiger who came to Tea* shows, it *is* possible.

● **Photocopiable page 26 'What strange weather we have'**
Following the previous activity, present the children with the scenario of a weather reporter who has lost her notes. She has to do the broadcast from memory, but is having a little difficulty. Show the children the table indicating how certain she is of the weather forecast in different parts of the country. Then ask them to use appropriate modal verbs to rewrite her report.

● **Photocopiable page 27 'Walter the wizard'**
This sheet builds on work done in Year 5 on adverbs and in Year 6 on modal verbs and adverbs. In this activity, children use cloze procedure to build up a story about a wizard who is developing a new spell but does not know what will happen when he tries it out.

Further ideas

● **Why did you do that?:** Following on from 'What strange weather we have', give the children the scenario that the boss of the television station, Mrs Green, has seen Wendy's weather report. She is not at all pleased with it and has asked Wendy to go to her office to explain. The children need to write what Wendy would say using modal verbs to show the choices that she had. She might start with: *Well, my computer crashed and I knew I wouldn't be able to get it working again in time. I could have just told the viewers that I had no idea about the weather but I thought that might not be the best thing to do so…* This is also an opportunity to expand the children's understanding by using modals in a negative way.

Digital content

On the digital component you will find:
● Printable versions of all three photocopiable pages.
● Answers to 'How likely is it?' and 'Walter the wizard'.

Modal verbs and adverbs

How likely is it?

Modal verbs can help us to understand how likely it is that something will happen. The table below shows you which modal verb to use to describe how possible something is.

Certainty	must will can shall
Probable	would ought to should
Possible	could might may

■   The following sentences all have modal verbs missing. Choose a modal verb that will make sense and write it in the space. The first one is done for you.

1. A tiger _____*could*_____ come for tea.

2. If today is Monday, then tomorrow _____ be Tuesday.

3. We _____ tell the truth all of the time.

4. It _____ rain all next week.

■   Write your own sentences, missing out a modal verb. Then ask a partner to fill in the gaps and see whether you agree with them or not.

_____

_____

_____

_____

_____

_____

Name:

What strange weather we have

Wendy is a TV weather reporter. She is due to give her forecast now, but she has lost some of her notes! She will have to do this part of the broadcast from memory. The table below shows how certain she is of the weather forecast in different parts of the country.

	Hot and sunny	Rainy	Windy	Thunderstorms
North		Possible	Probable	
Scotland				Probable
South	Probable			
South West	Certain			
Midlands		Possible		

■ Rewrite Wendy's weather report, using appropriate modal verbs to show how certain she is of the weather in each area. This has been started for you.

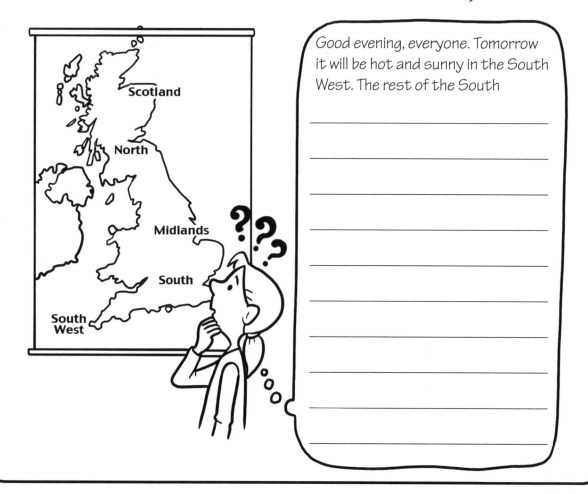

Good evening, everyone. Tomorrow it will be hot and sunny in the South West. The rest of the South

_____

_____

_____

_____

_____

_____

_____

_____

_____

Modal verbs and adverbs

Walter the wizard

Walter is practising to be a wizard. He has made up a new spell he hopes will turn wood into gold and make him rich. However, this is a new spell so he does not know what will happen.

■ Choose adverbs and modal verbs from the box to complete the story below. You can only use each word once and you do not need to use all of the words.

> **Adverbs:** always   only   never   ever   still   just   perhaps   surely
> **Modal verbs:** will   would   can   could   may   might   shall   should   must   ought

Walter had _____ (adverb) wanted to be a wizard. He

knew that he _____ (modal verb) be a great one. Walter

_____ (adverb) had the answer to his dreams when he invented

the 'goldspell'. He had wondered what would happen if he _____

(adverb) dared to try it but what _____ (modal verb) go wrong?

Worrying had _____ (adverb) stopped him before. Perhaps he

_____ (modal verb) find a way to test it. It _____

(adverb) needed to work once and then he would be rich! He made up his mind.

He _____ (adverb) had to say the magic words and see what

_____ (modal verb) happen.

Writing with verbs

Objective

Use verb forms and verb tenses correctly and consistently in writing and use verbs and adverbs to indicate degrees of possibility.

Writing focus

Building on previous activities, this section offers children the chance to use different verb tenses and forms and to explore the potential use of these in their writing.

Skills to writing

● Almost too tense for words

Ask the children to focus on writing in one specific tense, for example the past perfect. Present them with the scenario that they have been late for school and have to explain to their teacher the reasons, using the past perfect. For example: *We had got up in plenty of time and we had eaten our toast. We had packed our bags and we had started out for school. Unfortunately, we hadn't checked the bus timetable, so we didn't know that it had changed.*

Encourage the children to be aware of, and later check, that they are consistently using the appropriate tenses and are ensuring subject–verb agreement at all times.

● Model the modals

Ask the children to use their completed copies of photocopiable page 30 'Planning with modals' as the starting point for writing the ends of two stories. Each one must follow the plan on the sheet and end with a cliffhanger sentence that includes a modal verb. For example: *He turned to his mother. It was time she knew the truth. He **ought** to be the one to tell her.*

Activities

● Photocopiable page 30 'Planning with modals'

This activity inspires creative writing as the children are asked to devise possible alternative endings for a story, using modal verbs to guide them. They are encouraged to include adverbs in their planning to add more detail.

● Photocopiable page 31 'Irregular verbs'

This activity focuses on the past perfect and present perfect forms but this time it is using irregular verb endings. The children are given examples of irregular past participles. They are then asked to fill in a grid with more irregular past participles. Finally, they have to use the irregular past participles in past perfect or present perfect sentences and show their understanding by identifying them.

Write on

● Walter the wizard

Use photocopiable page 27 'Walter the wizard' as the starting point for an extended writing activity. Ask the children to use the original opening paragraph and to continue the story, showing what happened when he tried to test his spell. This can also be an opportunity to show how more than one tense can be used to add variety and to clarify meaning, such as past perfect with past, present perfect, present or present continuous.

● Irregular verbs

Ask the children to work in groups to make irregular verb tables that include the verb, its present form and its past participle.

● I could, I might, I ought

Present the children with a number of scenarios that require them to say what they would do, for example: *You find a purse in the street. What would you do?* Explain that their answers must include modal verbs, such as: *I ought to take it to the police station and hand it in*, or *I might take it home and give it to my mother*, or *I might feel bad, but I would keep it.*

Here are possible scenarios:

● You get blamed for something your best friend has done.

● You have forgotten your best friend's birthday.

● You are dropped from the school's football team.

● Your parents say you can have anything you want for your birthday.

Ask the children to write a short answer including at least one modal verb. In pairs, they should then discuss their answers and choose one to extend into a longer collaborative piece that shows the effects of their decisions.

● **The adverbs came too**

Adapt the previous activity 'I could, I might, I ought', this time asking the children to include an adverb as well.

For example: *You find a purse on the street, what would you do?* This time the answer could be: *Even though I know I should take it to the police station, I never would do it.*

Here are possible scenarios:

● You see someone shoplifting.

● You are late for school.

● Your best friend's parents ask you to go on holiday with them but your parents don't want you to go.

● Your favourite band is playing in your town but you can't afford to go.

As before, the children should write a short answer including at least one modal verb and an adverb. They should then choose one of the scenarios and extend this writing into a longer piece that develops the original by showing the effects of their decisions.

> ### Digital content
>
> On the digital component you will find:
>
> ● Printable versions of both photocopiable pages.
>
> ● Answers to 'Irregular verbs'.

Name:

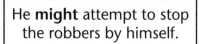
Writing with verbs

Planning with modals

■ Look at the example story plan below.
The three boxes suggest what could
happen in the final paragraph.

Jez has seen a robbery taking place.

He **might** attempt to stop the robbers by himself.
He **ought** to call the police on his mobile phone.
He **could** video the robbers on his phone.

■ You will now plan the end of a different story. In the three boxes below, write
what you think could happen in the final paragraph. Use the modal verb in each
box to guide you on how likely your ending might be.
■ Add detail to your planning by including one of these adverbs in each box.

always	only	never	ever	still	just	perhaps	surely

Tara sees her best friend cheating in the English reading test.

She **might**	She **ought**	She **can**
_____	_____	_____
_____	_____	_____
_____	_____	_____
_____	_____	_____

PHOTOCOPIABLE   **SCHOLASTIC**
www.scholastic.co.uk

Writing with verbs

Irregular verbs

Many of our most frequently used verbs are irregular – so their past form does not end in 'ed'. This table gives you some examples.

Irregular verb	Past
to be	been
to hold	held
to bring	brought
to make	made
to read	read (sounds like red)

■ In the table below, write what you think are the correct past forms for the verbs.

Irregular verb	Past
to catch	
to fight	
to hear	
to think	

■ Now put each of the following verbs into a sentence using the past perfect or present perfect form. Circle which form it is. The first one is done for you.

Verb	Sentence	Form
to read	I have read Black Beauty.	Past perfect (Present perfect)
to be		Past perfect Present perfect
to bring		Past perfect Present perfect
to make		Past perfect Present perfect
to hear		Past perfect Present perfect
to think		Past perfect Present perfect

SCHOLASTIC
www.scholastic.co.uk   PHOTOCOPIABLE   Scholastic English Skills
Grammar and punctuation: Year 6   31

Chapter 2

Formal and informal speech and writing

Introduction

Every day we use a variety of speech types depending upon the situation. Almost instinctively, we modify our language, vocabulary, speech and writing to fit what we are doing and our audience. In this chapter, children will identify formal and informal speech and writing. They will explore synonyms and antonyms. They will examine the structures that are typical of formal speech and writing and those typical of speech. Finally, they will work on transcribing speech and using formal language in emails. For further practice, please see the 'Formal and informal speech and writing' section of the Year 6 workbook.

Poster notes

Is it right or wrong? (page 33)
This poster helps to explain what antonyms and synonyms are. It also shows that the same words have different antonyms and synonyms. Ask children to use the same format to devise their own antonym and synonym noticeboard.

What d'yer mean? (page 34)
This poster shows some of the features and structures of informal and formal speech and writing. The images of formally dressed and casually dressed people will help to illustrate the appropriate context for each style of writing and speech. Display the poster as a starting point for formal or informal work.

In this chapter

Synonyms and antonyms page 35	Understand how words are related by meaning as synonyms and antonyms.
Formal and informal language page 39	Understand when formal and informal language may be used.
Vocabulary in speech and writing page 43	Recognise the difference between vocabulary typical of informal speech and appropriate for formal speech and writing.
Features of formal and informal language page 47	Recognise the difference between structures typical of informal speech and those appropriate for formal speech and writing.
Really writing page 51	Apply the features of formal and informal language to writing.

Vocabulary

Children should already know:
tense (past, present, perfect), direct speech, inverted commas, speech marks
In Year 6 children need to know:
synonym, antonym, subjunctive

Formal and informal speech and writing

Is it right or wrong?

A **synonym** is a word that means the same or almost the same as another word.
An **antonym** is a word that means the opposite of another word.

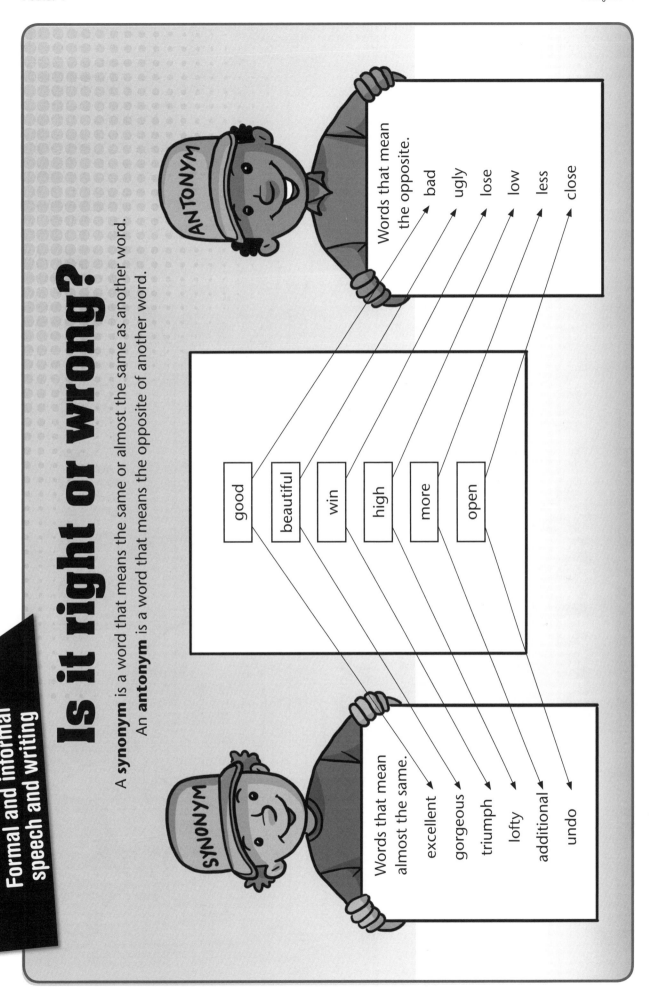

ANTONYM

Words that mean the opposite.

bad
ugly
lose
low
less
close

good
beautiful
win
high
more
open

SYNONYM

Words that mean almost the same.

excellent
gorgeous
triumph
lofty
additional
undo

What d'yer mean?

Formal speech or writing is used when we have prepared what we will say or write.

Letters of application	Standard English
Speeches	Thought out ideas
Answers in examinations	Structured sentences, paragraphs and accurate punctuation
Newspaper reports	

Informal speech or writing is used when we have not prepared what we will say or write.

Talking to friends	Non-standard English
At home	Spontaneous
Answering questions	Not structured
Texting	
Notes	

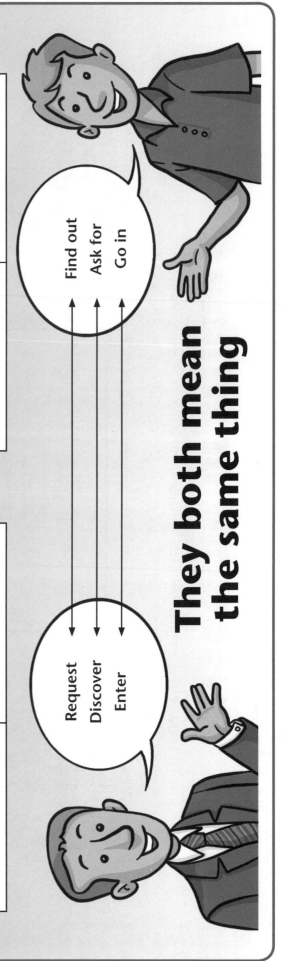

Request	Find out
Discover	Ask for
Enter	Go in

They both mean the same thing

PHOTOCOPIABLE

Synonyms and antonyms

Objective

Understand how words are related by meaning as synonyms and antonyms.

Background knowledge

Synonyms are words with similar meanings and antonyms have the opposite meanings. They are particularly useful to help children choose varied vocabulary that is appropriate for the context. The phrase 'synonyms are similar' will be a helpful way for children to remember which term is which. Remind the children that it's not just adjectives that can be synonyms or antonyms; verbs, nouns and adverbs can be, too.

Activities

● **Photocopiable page 36 'Matching pairs'**
This is a fun game that requires the children to recognise and understand synonyms by matching pairs of words. Explain that they must find words that mean the same as each other and pair them up. Once they have played the game, invite the children to demonstrate their understanding by working in pairs to create their own version of the game, with new words. They can then challenge another pair to play their game.

● **Photocopiable page 37 'Dear Gran'**
This sheet requires the children to demonstrate their understanding of antonyms. The children are asked to imagine they have received an awful pair of mittens for their birthday from their grandmother. They are given the text for a thank you note, explaining how they really feel. Invite them to think of appropriate antonyms to write a more tactful note. They could use a thesaurus for this activity.

● **Photocopiable page 38 'Read all about it!'**
Explain to the children that they are working to a deadline to complete the school newsletter on time, however, the reporter is ill and they only have ten minutes to write the final article using his notes. The notes are written using informal language, which the children must adapt to the formal tone of the newsletter, choosing appropriate synonyms.

Further ideas

● **Class thesaurus:** Split the class into groups and ask each group to use a thesaurus to look up commonly used synonyms for one of these words: 'good', 'bad', 'near', 'far', 'success', 'failure', 'friend', 'enemy', 'walk' and 'run'. Invite each group to make one page of the thesaurus, featuring the word, its definition, a list of synonyms and an example sentence to demonstrate its use. The children could then choose their own words to add.

● **Community thesaurus:** Use the same technique to add these words to the thesaurus: 'illness', 'truancy', 'head teacher', 'grassing', 'food' and 'money'. However, this time encourage the children to ask parents, grandparents, teachers and so on for synonymous words from their childhood. Collate the work into a booklet and display it.

● **Synonym circle:** Sit the children in a circle. Choose a verb such as 'fell'. As you go round the circle, each child must give a synonym for the verb. When a child cannot think of an answer, start the process again with an adjective and then a noun. You could use words from the class thesaurus. Alternatively, this could be used as a starting point for making one.

● **Sophie Synonym and Antony Antonym:** Give the children a piece of writing and explain that Sophie and Antony would like to improve it. Sophie wants to rewrite the piece using synonyms, and Antony wants to use antonyms. However, neither can think of any appropriate words. Ask the children to choose whether they want to help Sophie or Antony. They should then make lists of possible words to replace adjectives in the text and, finally, choose one word for each of them.

Digital content

On the digital component you will find:
● Printable versions of all three photocopiable pages.
● Answers to 'Matching pairs'.
● Interactive version of 'Matching pairs'.

Name:

Synonyms and antonyms

Matching pairs

■ Cut out each of the words below.

■ Working with a partner, place each word face down in front of you. Take turns to find pairs of synonyms – words that mean the same thing or similar. The player who collects the most synonyms is the winner.

■ If you do not know the meaning of any of the words, use a dictionary to look it up.

huge	rich	ate	waited
laughed	broken	terrifying	giggled
ran	stopped	useless	gobbled
tumbled	paused	shattered	fell
scary	wealthy	already	enormous
handy	dashed	futile	before
empty	useful	halted	vacant

■ When you have finished playing, work with your partner to think of new pairs of synonyms to make your own matching game. Write the words in the grid below. Do not use any of the words from the grid above.

■ Share your new game with another pair and see how quickly they can complete it.

Synonyms and antonyms

Dear Gran

Your grandmother has bought you a really awful
pair of mittens for your birthday.
That's not the worst of your problems.
You now need to write a formal thank you note.
This is what you really think:

> Thank you for the **awful** mittens. I thought the **shocking** blue and
> green colour scheme was **revolting**. They make my hands look
> **ridiculous**, all **stumpy** and **short**. I am so **annoyed** that you bought the
> **horrible** things. I am incredibly **upset** that you managed to get them. I
> will **never** wear them. My friends will **hate** them too. I cannot imagine
> a **worse** present. I am **dreading** opening my present next year.

■ You do not want to upset your grandmother, so you need to rewrite the thank
you note. Choose appropriate antonyms for the spaces below to make it sound like
you are actually very pleased with them.

> Thank you for the _____ mittens. I thought
>
> the _____ blue and green colour scheme was
>
> _____. They make my hands look _____,
>
> all _____ and _____. I am so
>
> _____ that you bought the _____ things. I
>
> am incredibly _____ that you managed to get them. I will
>
> _____ wear them. My friends will _____
>
> them too. I cannot imagine a _____ present. I am
>
> _____ opening my present next year.

Name:

Read all about it!

Your school newsletter is due out today but Robin, your roving reporter, is ill. He has asked you to write up the final article using his notes.
Unfortunately, when you find his notes you discover that they are very informal.

> Met <u>old Ma</u> Jones. Lives in the <u>old folks'</u> home opposite the school. Bit <u>narky</u> today. Too many kids causing a <u>racket</u> in her street after school. <u>Reckons</u> they want <u>sorting out</u>. Her <u>old feller</u> wouldn't have let them <u>carry on</u> like that. She's been on the <u>blower</u> to the <u>Old Bill</u>. They say they've got too much <u>on their plates</u> to do <u>owt</u>. <u>Nowt's</u> going to change. If it doesn't get better she's going to give <u>some</u> <u>bloke</u> at the council <u>some earache</u>.

■ Write up this short article using formal language, which is more appropriate for a newsletter for the teachers, parents and children at your school.

■ Think of suitable synonyms for the words and phrases that are underlined.

■ Work quickly as you only have ten minutes before the newsletter needs to be printed! Write it on a separate sheet of paper.

Wednesday, October 15, Scholastic Daily

Local resident is shocked by children's behaviour

Formal and informal language

Objective

Understand when formal and informal language may be used.

Background knowledge

Both speech and writing may use informal and formal language. The key to knowing which to use is in the context. Formal or official documents have certain characteristics that distinguish them from a friendly note or an informal narrative. They commonly use impersonal subjects to refer to people, such as *the vendor* or *the proprietor*. They may also use specific terminology and phrases, such as *in the eventuality* instead of *should*. At times, this formal structure and choice of vocabulary may actually obscure the meaning of a text.

The choice of speech or writing depends upon the situation. You are unlikely to send a formal letter asking the supermarket manager for a tin of beans. In contrast, the supermarket manager would not offer you a job without a written contract. The important thing is to know when and how to use both forms.

Activities

● **Photocopiable page 40 'Everything has its place'**
This is a sorting activity. Cut the scenarios out and ask the children to work in pairs to place each under one of four titles: formal writing, informal writing, formal speech and informal speech.

● **Photocopiable page 41 'Who writes what?'**
Invite the children to match the examples of different texts to their descriptions. Ask them to look out for levels of formality and clues within the language to decide which text is which.

● **Photocopiable page 42 'Let's talk about it'**
Ask the children to explore the language used in different jobs. Can they say how likely people would be to use formal or informal language in different jobs? Working in groups, they should focus on one job, creating a spider diagram on a large sheet of paper, listing the reasons for their decision and examples of the language someone doing this job might use.

Further ideas

● **Which side are you on?:** Stick the word 'Informal' on one classroom wall and 'Formal' on the opposite side. Distribute the cards from photocopiable page 42 'Let's talk about it' to members of the class. Ask four children who have not been given cards to come to the front. The children with the cards take it in turns to read out the jobs on them. The children at the front have to move to the appropriate side of the classroom. The remaining children who do not have cards then have to decide if the others have moved to the correct label.

● **Don't say 'Erm':** Divide the class into two teams of roughly equal ability. Give the children a topic, such as 'assembly'. Do not give them any preparation time. Ask one child to speak in a formal manner on the subject for 20 seconds without stopping. Children in the other team can challenge if they think the child is hesitating, going off the subject or not speaking in a formal way. When a challenge is made, the timer is paused. If the challenge is correct, the challenger takes over and tries to complete the remaining time. The child who is speaking at the end of the 20 seconds wins a point for their team.

● **Who would say a thing like that?:** Using the jobs from photocopiable page 42 'Let's talk about it', give the children a typical statement someone in one of the jobs might say. Let the children write which job they think it is on an individual whiteboard and hold it up to show you. Alternatively, read out a job and a statement. Ask the children to put a tick or a cross on their whiteboard, to indicate whether they think the person would have said it or not. For example: *I am a judge. Would I say, 'You're going down, my mate', to the prisoner?* If the statement didn't match, ask the children to write down what the person would have said instead.

Digital content

On the digital component you will find:
● Printable versions of all three photocopiable pages.
● Answers for all three photocopiable pages.
● Interactive version of 'Who writes what?'.

Name:

Formal and informal language

Everything has its place

■ Cut out the situations below.

✂

Letting your friend know you will be five minutes late	An application for a job	Making a complaint to your local MP
The prime minister answering questions in Parliament	Asking for directions	Recording the main points to help you revise
Letting the public know the latest facts in a news story	A job interview	A shopping list
Planning this task with your partner	A contract for a job	Catching up with friends
Letting people in your area know your cat is missing	A message to your cousin in Australia	A radio traffic report

■ Work in pairs to place each situation under one of the four forms of communication listed below.

Formal writing	**Informal writing**
Formal speech	**Informal speech**

■ Discuss with your partner whether any of the situations could be put in more than one box and why that could be.

■ Devise other situations and share them with another pair. See if they agree with you.

PHOTOCOPIABLE

■SCHOLASTIC
www.scholastic.co.uk

Formal and informal language

Who writes what?

- Read each piece of text and match it to the correct description.
- Cut out and match up pairs. Then stick them onto a sheet of paper.

Am I the only reader who is angry about the road works in the centre of town?	Round at Josh's. See you at 5.00.	I have had a good weekend, reading books and watching television. Very relaxing.
WISH YOU WERE HERE. THE SUN IS BRILLIANT!	It is of the utmost importance that you contact me as soon as possible to discuss your financial arrangements.	Take a look at our brochure. We offer sun, sea and adventure. Whatever you are looking for next **summer – we'll look after you**.
It was just what I wanted and I was so surprised. Thanks again, Sam.	Oh, Juliet. You are like the sun. Please, please reply soon.	

Descriptions

Letter of complaint to a local newspaper	A love letter!
Letter from a bank manager to someone who owes the bank money	Letter from a holiday company advertising their holidays
A text between two friends	Note left on the fridge from a boy to his mum
Postcard from a holiday	Thank you letter from a child to his granny

Name:

Formal and informal language

Let's talk about it

■ Working in groups, cut out the cards below and place them face downwards on the table.

■ Pick three cards and discuss them together as a group. Decide whether people in these jobs are more likely to use formal or informal language in their job.

■ Choose one of the three jobs and make a spider diagram to show your reasons.

■ Expand your spider diagram to include examples of what someone doing this job might say.

Police officer	Gardener	Solicitor
Security guard	News reporter	Decorator
Taxi driver	Professional footballer	Doctor
Mechanic	Teacher in assembly	Builder
Judge	Window cleaner	Lorry driver

Vocabulary in speech and writing

Objective

Recognise the difference between vocabulary typical of informal speech and appropriate for formal speech and writing.

Background knowledge

Formal and informal speech and writing have different structures and vocabulary, such as the use the subjunctive form (*If I were…*), register (varieties of a language related to a range of uses, such as novels and newspaper reports) or question tags (*That's right, isn't it?*). The children need to be able to differentiate between formal and informal styles and be able to use them appropriately.

Activities

● **Photocopiable page 44 'Say it or write it?'**
Two types of sentence are shown, each saying something similar, but one is more formal. Ask the children to match the sentences and decide which sentences are more likely to be written and which are more likely to be spoken. They should justify their reasoning for two of the sentences. Encourage the children to identify what sort of vocabulary differentiates the two types of communication.

● **Photocopiable page 45 'Right words, right occasion'**
Language reflects the context in which it is used. As children approach the various scenarios on this sheet, they should be challenged to imagine how these people would speak. How will the use of vocabulary and sentence type reflect the attitude of the speaker?

● **Photocopiable page 46 'Word train'**
In this activity, the children must decide which phrases on the 'Word train' should be delivered to one of three stations. When they have written each phrase on to the station nameplates, they will have created three different versions of the same message. Encourage the children to work in pairs to discuss how they were able to recognise each type of communication.

Further ideas

● **Put it to use:** Using the sentences from photocopiable page 44 'Say it or write it?', ask the children to decide what sort of vocabulary differentiates the two types of communication. You could extend this further by asking the children to give examples of where and when each sentence would be used. Ask the children to write a short letter including the phrase *Your behaviour was inappropriate* and a short playscript including the phrase *You were mucking about*.

● **Collect formalities:** Ask children to collect formal notices and letters from adults and look at some of the language used in them. Look at letters of various kinds along with postcards, emails and junk mail. Encourage children to try rewriting these in their own words.

● **Contract writing:** Invite the children to draw up their own contracts between two different parties, such as an agreement to keep the classroom tidy.

Digital content

On the digital component you will find:
● Printable versions of all three photocopiable pages.
● Answers to 'Say it or write it?' and 'Word train'.

Name:

Say it or write it?

- Cut out the sentences below.
- Match pairs of sentences with similar meanings.
- For each pair of sentences, decide which is more likely to be used in speech and which is more likely to be used in writing.

You were mucking about.	Please leave immediately.	That telly programme was great.	I went to the loo.
I used the bathroom.	Your behaviour was inappropriate.	I'd love another plate of pudding.	Go away now.
Thank you for inviting me to your house.	Cheers for asking me round.	The television programme was immensely enjoyable.	The room had a terrible smell.
I sure was glad when the racket stopped.	I would have enjoyed a further helping of the sweet course.	The place stank something shocking.	It was a huge relief when the noise finally ended.

- Choose one sentence that is more likely to be used in speech and explain why.

Sentence: _____

Reason: _____

- Choose one sentence that is more likely to be used in writing and explain why.

Sentence: _____

Reason: _____

PHOTOCOPIABLE **SCHOLASTIC** www.scholastic.co.uk

Vocabulary in speech and writing

Right words, right occasion

■ Here are four different occasions. How will the people in each situation speak? What is different about the way they will talk?

This man is taking a pair of trousers that were too small back to the shop. How will he talk?

This man has just been served food that was cold. How will he talk?

This girl is meeting the prime minister. How will she talk?

This boy is making a speech to the whole school. How will he talk?

SCHOLASTIC
www.scholastic.co.uk   **PHOTOCOPIABLE**   **Scholastic English Skills**
Grammar and punctuation: Year 6   **45**

Name:

Word train

The word train is delivering useful words to the different stations along its route. Each truck has three different phrases on it.

■ Write the phrases from each truck that you think are most appropriate on each station nameplate.

| Dear Sir/Madam

Dear Charlie

Hi there | Let's meet Tuesday.

I'd like to arrange a meeting for Tuesday.

Can we meet next Tuesday? | Would 3pm be convenient?

How about 3-ish?

Will 3pm be OK? | See you then!

I'll see you next week.

I look forward to seeing you soon. |

Formal writing

Informal writing

Informal speech

Features of formal and informal language

Recognise the difference between structures typical of informal speech and those appropriate for formal speech and writing.

Background knowledge

The subjunctive form is used more in writing. It is used when we are writing about things that we want to happen, that we imagine will happen, or, that we expect to happen. For example, *It's crucial that you be at the bus by 5pm.*

In the past tense 'were' is used instead of 'was'. For example: *If I were in charge, we would have longer holidays.* But I am not in charge, so we use 'were' instead of 'was'.

In the present tense 'be' is used instead of 'am', 'are' or 'is'. For example: *Mr Jones demands that his children be silent.* But this is not always the case so we use 'be' rather than 'are'.

The subjunctive can also use 'that'. Verb + 'that' – *to advise that*, *to ask that*, *to command that*, *to demand that*, *to insist that*, *to propose that*, *to recommend that*, *to request that*, *to suggest that*.

After phrases + 'that' – it *is essential that*, *it is desirable that*, *it is vital that.* These can all be followed by 'that' and an action.

Question tags are used almost solely in speech. They are a way of encouraging our listeners to agree with us, such as *You agree, don't you?*

Activities

● **Photocopiable page 48 'Structures'**
This activity focuses on the subjunctive form and question tags. Ask the children to fill in the gaps in the sentences with appropriate subjunctives or question tags. They must be careful to use the subjunctive each time. For example: *It is important that you are smartly dressed for interviews* is not in the subjunctive form. The correct answer would be *It is important that you be smartly dressed for interviews.* The sheet asks them

to explain how they know the sentences are in the subjective form (they use the simple form of the verb 'to be', creating a more formal impression), and to explain the effect of using question tags.

● **Photocopiable page 49 'How would you write this?'**
This activity provides two texts that include examples of the breaks and flows of speech. The unpunctuated and staccato nature of these texts should contrast with the written sentences that the children produce. They should be able to explain the differences.

● **Photocopiable page 50 'Wedding invitation'**
This activity gives the children two examples of formal writing. The children are asked to use this information to compose an informal email in reply.

Further ideas

● **Relaxed and formal dialogue:** As a drama activity, ask the children to work in pairs to devise either an informal situation into which they inject formal dialogue, or a formal situation that they act out with informal speech. For example, they could improvise a scene in court where a police officer is giving evidence and quoting what the defendant had said. The children should think about the structures and vocabulary they will use.

● **Is it all right to say this?:** Divide the children into groups and give them the words: 'friend', 'home', 'mother', 'father', 'toilet', 'food', 'beautiful', 'clever'. Ask half of the groups to devise informal synonyms and the other half to find formal ones. Finally, list antonyms and discuss why some words are harder to find antonyms for, such as 'toilet'.

Digital content

On the digital component you will find:
● Printable versions of all three photocopiable pages.
● Answers to 'Structures'.

Name:

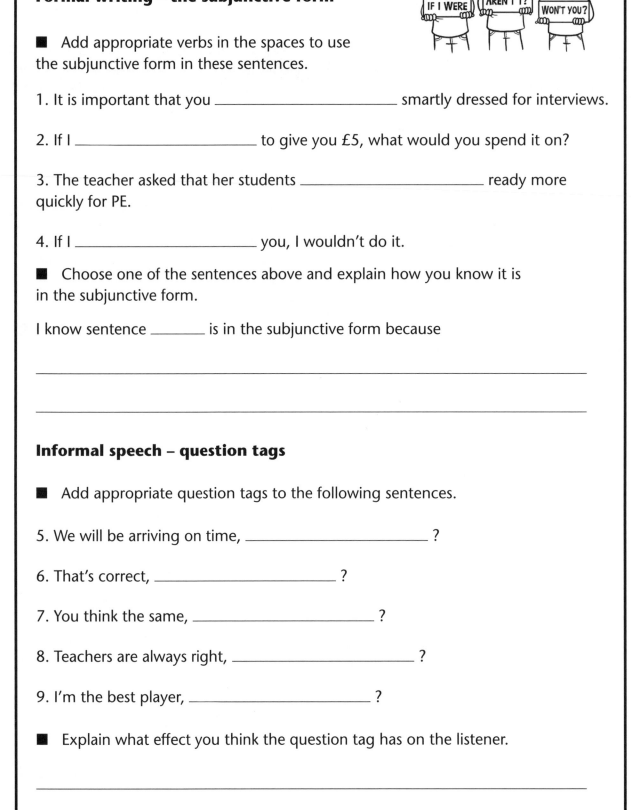

Features of formal and informal language

Structures

Formal writing – the subjunctive form

■ Add appropriate verbs in the spaces to use the subjunctive form in these sentences.

1. It is important that you _____ smartly dressed for interviews.

2. If I _____ to give you £5, what would you spend it on?

3. The teacher asked that her students _____ ready more quickly for PE.

4. If I _____ you, I wouldn't do it.

■ Choose one of the sentences above and explain how you know it is in the subjunctive form.

I know sentence _____ is in the subjunctive form because

_____

_____

Informal speech – question tags

■ Add appropriate question tags to the following sentences.

5. We will be arriving on time, _____ ?

6. That's correct, _____ ?

7. You think the same, _____ ?

8. Teachers are always right, _____ ?

9. I'm the best player, _____ ?

■ Explain what effect you think the question tag has on the listener.

_____

_____

How would you write this?

These transcripts show exactly what two people said.

- Rewrite one of them using formal writing.
- Rewrite the other using informal writing.

> Oh Sara listen…listen… tell you what I was thinking, like d'ya think it'd be ok for us to do our story on your computer cos mines all bust and my mum says it ain't gonna get fixed until after pay day and its sort of awkward cos we gotta get this thing done, yeh?

> Miss, miss, let me tell you about Saturday cos me and Carlos we found this bubble wrap and really big bubbles it was — all of it so we took us shoes and socks off and we walked all over it and, like, dug our heels in and pop pop pop it was like fireworks and then we started jumping on it and it was a real laugh.

- Explain the differences in the structure and vocabulary between your versions and the original ones.

_____

_____

_____

Name:

Wedding invitation

You have received the following wedding invitation.

Mr and Mrs Harold Worth request the pleasure of your company
to celebrate the marriage of their daughter

Fiona Alison

to

Mr Thomas Cooper

*at 2pm on Saturday 22 July
and afterwards at the Royal Hotel, Brompton.*

RSVP 47 Tolpuddle Lane
Brompton BR5 6TD

You had written a formal response, accepting the invitation, but then forgot to post it! The deadline for replying is today.

Dear Mr and Mrs Worth
Thank you very much for your invitation to attend
the wedding of Fiona and Thomas. I am delighted
to accept and I am looking forward to the occasion.
Yours faithfully

■ You decide to send Mr and Mrs Worth an informal email instead. Write your response in the space below.

_____

_____

_____

_____

Really writing

Objective

Apply the features of formal and informal language to writing.

Writing focus

Building on previous activities, this section encourages children to experiment with the conventions of formal language and to consider the features of informal language in speech.

Skills to writing

- **Language in context**

Following the work done in this chapter, children should be encouraged to listen out for language in contexts and tune in to the ways people write and speak, depending on the circumstances. Ask the children to write brief, informal notes as if taken by a reporter at the scene of a burglary. They could then write them up as a formal piece for a newspaper article.

- **At home**

Focusing on language use, give the children the following statements:

- Posh people don't talk better than other people.
- On TV, people speak differently on serious programmes.
- At school, they really don't teach you how to speak.
- You speak better as you get older.

Ask the children to take some of these ideas home and find out what their families think. They should then choose one of the scenarios and write a short response.

- **This is the news**

You can do this activity when a major event takes place in your school, such as sports day or the Christmas concert. Divide the children into groups and allocate them areas of the subject on which to write a short formal report. They will have to script formal pieces for the start of the programme but more informal 'to camera' pieces and interviews. You could be really adventurous by making a video of the event, including interviews with participants, and showing them as part of your report. For example, children could record the 100 metres race, then script the report that the 'on the spot reporter' would make. They should finish this off with an informal interview with the winner at the end of the race. If you do choose to record this, it could be presented as a news broadcast to the whole school.

- **You're going to need to know this**

This will allow you to assess the children's understanding of the work they have done in this chapter. Tell the children that they are going to make a presentation for the Year 5 children in your school. Divide the children into groups and ask them to create posters in a formal style to explain each of the elements they have covered.

Activities

- **Photocopiable page 53 'What did you say?'**

In this activity, children record and use speech as a starting point for writing. They will need to practise transcribing speech, word for word, but once they have done this they can produce the comparative forms. Ask them to record a partner telling a factual story and then transcribe it exactly. Using the transcript, they must then write the story in the form of a formal newspaper report. They can use informal language in this, but only if they are quoting their partner.

- **Photocopiable page 54 'Formal emails'**

Using the email banners on the sheet, invite the children to step into one of the roles outlined and write a formal email suitable for their chosen scenario. Encourage them to anticipate questions their addressee will raise and tackle any objections before they are raised. For example, how might the head teachers react to having shorter holidays? Remind the children of the need to write in a formal style. They could work in pairs to discuss the structures of formal writing from this chapter that they might include. They could also create the finished product electronically.

Write on

● **The language of...**

An investigation that can be written up involves exploring the language of certain fields of life. Football playing and reporting has a particular semantic field that is different to the one encountered in the world of pop music. What about car enthusiasts or horse fanatics? Ask children to work in groups exploring, collating and explaining the language peculiar to different fields.

● **Thesaurus work**

Ask the children to write a definition of informal writing to go on the classroom wall. Then invite them to look up the words from their definition in a thesaurus and rewrite the definition as if it were for a dictionary. Following on from this, ask the children to write individual explanations of what informal writing is and when it should be used. They should include some short examples to support their points.

● **I have a dream**

Read an extract of Martin Luther King's 'I have a dream' speech. This was written to be spoken formally. Ask the children to imagine their perfect school and to list all of its attributes. Then ask them to write a formal speech starting with *I have a dream*. They should write it as if they are presenting it to the prime minister.

Digital content

On the digital component you will find:
● Printable versions of both photocopiable pages.

Really writing

What did you say?

■ Make a recording of one of your friends telling you a true short story about themselves. You could do this on a mobile phone or with a video camera.

■ Play the recording back and find a section that is really interesting. In the 'Transcript' box below, copy out exactly what they said, word for word, including any fillers such as 'er', 'um' and 'erm'.

■ In the 'Newspaper report' box, write up their story as if it were in your local newspaper. You will need to use formal language unless you are quoting exactly what they have said, using speech marks.

Transcript	Newspaper report

■ Choose some of the informal words that you replaced with formal words for the news report and explain the difference you think they have made.

I changed _____ to _____

The difference it made was

_____

_____

■ SCHOLASTIC
www.scholastic.co.uk   **PHOTOCOPIABLE**   **Scholastic English Skills**
Grammar and punctuation: Year 6   **53**

Name:

Formal emails

Formal emails will often have an official headed banner across the top.

■ Cut out and use one of the email banners below to create your own formal response, as described in the 'email brief'.

The Broadcasting Corporation

TBC

Email brief:

You are a producer making a new pop show. You are writing to a pop star to ask them on the show and tell them what you want.

Premier Association

Email brief:

You are a manager setting up a new football team. You are writing to another manager to try and buy some of his or her players, but you can't afford to pay the full price.

The prime minister's office

Email brief:

You are the prime minister and you have decided to shorten the school holidays. You are writing to all head teachers to inform them.

Chapter 3

Complexities in sentences

Introduction

This chapter deals with some of the more complex areas of the Programmes of Study. The main focus is on the use of the active voice and the passive voice. The children will learn to transpose sentences from one voice to the other. To enable them to do this, they will learn how to recognise the subject and the object of sentences. For further practice, please see the 'Complexities in sentences' section of the Year 6 workbook.

Poster notes

Active and passive (page 56)
This poster presents the way in which sentences written in the active voice can be transformed into the passive. The process can be shared in a whole-class reading of the poster but should be followed with children's attempts to make the change for themselves. It does not deal with the question of what the subject becomes when it moves to the end of the sentence in the passive. This is called a preposition phrase but the children are not required to know this in the Programmes of Study for Year 6.

Active and passive sentences (page 57)
The sentences on this poster contain verbs in the active and passive voice. No pointers are given as to which is which. Ask the children to try to identify the different types of verb voice for themselves. They can also try to change sentences written in one voice into another.

In this chapter

Getting verbs right page 58	Identify the subject and object of a sentence.
Active and passive page 62	Understand the terms active and passive.
Forming the passive page 66	Use the passive to affect the presentation of information in a sentence.
Relative clauses page 70	Use relative clauses beginning with 'who', 'which', 'where', 'when', 'whose', 'that' or with an implied (omitted) relative pronoun.
Writing in the active and passive voice page 74	Write sentences and texts in both the active and passive voice.

Vocabulary

Children should already know:
tense (past, present), clause, subordinate clause
In Year 6 children need to know:
active, passive, subject, object, relative clause

Complexities in sentences

Active and passive

Actions can be written in the active voice or the passive voice.

In the **active voice** the action in the verb is done by a subject to an object:

The school *(subject)* **arranged** *(verb)* **a visit** *(object)*.

In the **passive voice**, the object moves to the front of the sentence to become the subject.

A visit *(subject)* **was arranged** *(verb)* **by the school.**

The **visit** has moved to the front of the sentence and become the subject.

When the passive is used, the verb has either **was** or **were** placed in front of it, and **by** placed after it.

Scholastic English Skills
Grammar and punctuation: Year 6

PHOTOCOPIABLE

SCHOLASTIC
www.scholastic.co.uk

Complexities in sentences

Active and passive sentences

The children were chased by the dog.

Sam made this cake.

This cake was made by Sam.

The dog chased the children.

The boy found the keys.

The keys were found by the boy.

Getting verbs right

Objective

Identify the subject and object of a sentence.

Background knowledge

In a sentence, the subject is usually the person or the thing that does the action of the verb. For example, in *Sonja drives,* the verb is 'drives' and 'Sonja' is doing the driving so is the subject of the verb. If the sentence is extended to *Sonja drives her car*, the verb is still 'drives' and 'Sonja' is still the subject because she is still doing the driving. However, this sentence now contains an object. An object is the person or thing that has the action of the verb done to it. Now, 'her car' becomes the object because it is being driven. In the passive, the original object moves to the front of the sentence and becomes the subject. The original subject moves behind the verb, but it does not become the object. Instead, the word 'by' is inserted, creating a preposition phrase.

Activities

● **Photocopiable page 59 'Subject or object?'**
This exercise introduces the children to the subject and the object. It defines both terms and asks the children to identify them both in sentences. Their understanding is assessed by the explanations they give for their choices.
● **Photocopiable page 60 'Breaking down the sentences'**
This sheet encourages the analysis of verbs, leading to some interesting readings of various texts. The sentences increase in complexity and at the end the children are introduced to the idea of the implied subject, where the subject is not actually stated in the sentence. The children have to work out who or what the subject could be. Encourage children to move beyond the example sentences to other sentences from various texts, such as stories or their own writing.

● **Photocopiable page 61 'Doing or done?'**
This activity looks at active and passive voices without introducing children to the specific terms. They must decide if the person stated is the subject of each sentence. They need to ask whether the subject in bold is actively doing the action (*the **princess** saved the prince*) or having the action done to them (*the prince was saved by the **princess***). This activity provides a way of introducing the words 'active' and 'passive' by asking questions like: *Is the princess actively saving the prince? Is the prince passively being saved?* By correctly highlighting the objects and observing the different piles, the children should deduce that the sentences in the passive do not have any.

Further ideas

● **Photographic verbs:** Ask children to look at pictures of various actions or events in a newspaper and summarise each picture in a sentence. They can then look at the sentence to see if they can locate the verb, the subject and the object.
● **Who's the subject?:** Working in groups of three, ask the children to devise sentences that have a subject, a verb and an object, such as *Lesley stroked the cat*. One person reads out the sentence to the rest of the class. The other two act it out. The rest of the class have to correctly identify who the subject is and who or what the object is by deciding who is doing the action and who or what is having it done to them. They should also give reasons for their decisions.
● **Two subjects:** In pairs, ask the children to make up sentences with two subjects, two verbs and two objects in them. For example, *George and I walked to the shops where he bought some sweets*. They then share these sentences with another pair who have to identify the subjects, objects and verbs and give reasons for their thoughts.

Digital content

On the digital component you will find:
● Printable versions of all three photocopiable pages.
● Answers for all three photocopiable pages.
● Interactive versions of 'Subject or object' and 'Doing or done?'.

Getting verbs right

Subject or object?

■ In the sentences below, circle the subject.

1. Oliver ran to school.

2. Maggie kicked the football.

3. The teacher taught the class.

4. The mother washed her baby.

5. The dog chased the cat.

SUBJECT= does action

■ Choose one of the sentences and explain why you have chosen the word in it as the subject.

In sentence _____ I have chosen _____ as the subject because

_____

_____

■ In the following sentences, circle the object.

6. The football team won the tournament.

7. Jez walked his dog.

8. The twins shared their bedroom.

9. The gardener cut the grass.

10. The hairdresser cut my hair.

OBJECT= has action done do it

■ Choose one of the sentences and explain why you have chosen the word in it as the object.

In sentence _____ I have chosen _____ as the object because

_____

_____

Name:

Getting verbs right

Breaking down the sentences

■ Break down these sentences by spotting the verbs, subjects and objects within them. Then write them in the table below.

1. Prince Charming woke Sleeping Beauty.
2. Anne Frank wrote a diary.
3. Neil Armstrong went to the Moon.
4. Captain Cook discovered Australia.

Subject (who or what is doing the action)	Verb (the action)	Object (who or what is having the action done to them)

■ Sometimes sentences are more complicated. In this sentence there are two verbs, two subjects and two objects. Find them all and write them in the table.

5. The driver stopped the bus and the passengers left it.

Subject (who or what is doing the action)	Verb (the action)	Object (who or what is having the action done to them)

Sometimes the subject is not included in the sentence. It is implied and we simply understand it. For example, there is no subject stated in this sentence.

"Go to the head teacher's office."

■ Write what you think the subject could be and why you think that.

I think the subject could be _____ because

_____

_____

Getting verbs right

Doing or done?

■ The subject of each of the sentences below is in bold.

■ Circle the object in the sentences. Remember, not all of the sentences have objects.

■ Cut out the sentences and sort them into two groups:
- those in which the person in bold is doing the action
- those in which the action is done to the person in bold.

Callum helped Josh with his picture.	**Josh** was helped by Callum.
Lisa gave Danny his present.	**Danny** was given a present by Lisa.
Lisa was given a present by Danny.	**Danny** gave Lisa a present.
The princess saved the prince.	**The prince** was saved by the princess.
The burglar ran from the police.	**The burglar** was scared by the police car.
Jack was tripped up by Jill.	**Jill** tripped Jack up.
The policewoman chased the burglar.	**The burglar** was chased by the police.
Chloe lost her little sister in the supermarket.	**Chloe's little sister** was lost in the supermarket.
On Tuesday, **my uncle** went shopping.	**I** was bought a present by my uncle.

■ What do you notice about the objects and the verbs in the group in which something is done to the object?

_____

_____

Active and passive

Understand the terms active and passive.

Background knowledge

Sentences usually contain at least one verb. The subject of a sentence is the person or thing involved in that action. In a simple sentence like *Jack laughed* the subject is 'Jack' and the verb is 'laughed'.

Clauses can also include an object. This is the person or thing to whom the verb is done. For example: *Jack (subject) found (verb) his keys (object)*. This example is written in the active voice – the subject is actively doing the verb.

Alternatively, when written in the passive voice, the subject can be the one to whom the verb was done. For example: *The keys (subject) were found (verb) by Jack*. The object does not exist in the passive voice. The words 'by Jack' are a preposition phrase.

Activities

● **Photocopiable page 63 'Sentence flipping'**
In this activity, children read active sentences and then complete passive versions of them. As they remodel the sentences, stress that they should include all the information from the active sentence in their passive version. For example, in the sentence: *The fierce, little dog chased the children*, they need to include all the adjectives in their passive version: *The children were chased by the fierce, little dog*.

● **Photocopiable page 64 'Active or passive?'**
This sorting activity focuses on the active voice and passive voice, asking children to distinguish between the use of the two styles in a range of sentences. There is a similarity between a number of the examples, which means children have to look hard for the distinction between the active and passive.

● **Photocopiable page 65 'Use of the passive'**
This activity uses a range of texts from various contexts, asking the children to identify which ones are passive. The passive texts are the newspaper headline (because the hostages do not release themselves), the extract from the encyclopedia (because the focusing knob does not turn itself), and the extract from the advertisement (because the kitchens did not design themselves). Once the children have completed this, ask them to look at the extract about the microscope and consider how typical this is of explanatory sentences.

Further ideas

● **Text shading:** Ask the children to read a newspaper article and shade active sentences in red and passive sentences in blue. They can look at which is more common and see if this is a feature of one article or of the paper as a whole.

● **Sentence cutting:** Invite the children to write words on cards that will go together to make up a sentence in the active voice. They can challenge a partner to reconstruct the sentence. Ask them to create additional cards with 'by' and 'was' on them. They should then give this sentence and the additional cards to another pair to first make the active sentence and then the passive one using the additional cards.

● **When should we use them?:** In groups, ask the children to discuss occasions when they think that the active voice would be the better one to use and occasions when the passive voice would be better. The groups should prepare a two-minute presentation on this to give to the rest of the class, including examples. This will allow you to assess their understanding.

Digital content

On the digital component you will find:
● Printable versions of all three photocopiable pages.
● Answers for all three photocopiable pages.
● Interactive versions for all three photocopiable pages.

Active and passive

Sentence flipping

This sentence | The dog chased the cat. | can be flipped over so that the end

comes at the beginning: | The cat was chased by the dog. |

■ Finish the 'flipped' sentences below.

The cat chased the mouse.	The mouse was
My mum made this cake.	This cake
I found the keys.	The keys
We painted the large picture.	The large picture
Sam, Jake and Chloe tidied Gran's garden.	Gran's garden
Shona wrote the scary story.	The scary story
The fierce, little dog chased the children.	The children
All the teachers in our school wrote our school play.	Our school play
The shopkeeper and his children painted the front of the shop.	The front of the shop
Carlos glued and painted the model.	The model

■ SCHOLASTIC
www.scholastic.co.uk   **PHOTOCOPIABLE**   **Scholastic English Skills**
Grammar and punctuation: Year 6   **63**

Active and passive

Active or passive?

Actions can be written in the active voice or the passive voice.

In the active voice the action is done by a subject:

The lion *(subject)* **chased** *(verb)* **the zebra** *(object).*

In the passive voice the action is done to a subject:

The zebra *(subject)* **was chased** *(verb)* **by the lion.**

The subject is who or what did the action of the verb.

■   Cut out the cards and sort the sentences into active voice and passive voice.

The monster chased the goblin.	The window was broken by the football.
The goblin was chased by the monster.	Laura scored a goal.
Sam found the lost key.	The key was found by Sam.
The monster was chased by the goblin.	On Tuesday Mum went to town.
Sam lost the key.	The goblin chased the monster.
The boy made the sandwich.	The children performed the play.
The key was lost by Sam.	The sandwich was made by the boy.
A goal was scored by Laura.	The parents were entertained by the play.

Scholastic English Skills
64   Grammar and punctuation: Year 6   **PHOTOCOPIABLE**   ■ SCHOLASTIC
                                                                           www.scholastic.co.uk

Active and passive

Use of the passive

■ Look at these text extracts. Which of them are written in the active voice and which are written in the passive voice? Circle the appropriate answers.

Extract from a news report	The judge adjourned the case until next Wednesday.	Active Passive
Newspaper headline	Hostages released!	Active Passive
Extract from an advertisement	Our kitchens were designed by experts.	Active Passive
Extract from an encyclopedia explanation of a microscope	The focusing knob is turned by hand.	Active Passive
Extract from a complaint letter	We waited over an hour for the waitress to bring our pizza.	Active Passive
Extract from a conversation between two friends	"I saw Collette yesterday." "How was she?" "She was ill."	Active Passive

■ Write down some text extracts from books on the back of this sheet. Sort them into those that are active and those that are passive.

Forming the passive

Objective

Use the passive to affect the presentation of information in a sentence.

Background knowledge

The active voice has the usual pattern of subject and verb. The object in the active voice becomes the subject in the passive. A verb is not passive just because it has a passive meaning, it must be the passive version of an active verb.

Sentences can be altered from the active to the passive voice. Let's look at the example *Jack (subject) found (verb) his keys (object)*. The simplest way of understanding this process is by looking at how the verb changes. From the straightforward 'found', the passive form typically involves the addition of the word 'by' after the verb ('found by') and a form of the verbs 'be' ('was', 'is', 'are') or 'get' ('got') before the verb ('were found by').

Additionally, the object of the active form of the verb ('the keys') becomes the subject of the passive form. The passive form of the original sentence would be: *The keys (subject) were found (verb) by Jack.*

Activities

● **Photocopiable page 67 'Transforming sentences'**
In this activity the children are asked to make sentences passive, using the process outlined on the sheet. They need to change the tense of the verb, rearrange the subject and object around the verb, and add 'was' or 'were' and 'by' to show who did the action.
● **Photocopiable page 68 'Changing voices'**
To undertake this activity, children will need access to a range of texts. You may want to provide some leeway for children to simplify sentences in the active voice, picking out a particular clause from within a complex example. The main point of the activity is to get the children looking at how sentences and clauses in real life can be altered.

● **Photocopiable page 69 'Sentence switching'**
As children work through the examples, they should develop their skills of switching sentences from one voice to another. As they do this, they can also look at the sorts of changes they are making to various pieces of language to shape the transformation.

Further ideas

● **The reading scheme:** Looking at some of the reading books within school, children can try to alter the voice of the verbs throughout these texts. Reading schemes will provide a lot of examples of the active voice that children can switch to the passive voice.
● **Passive back:** As a whole-class activity, say a sentence in the active voice and ask the children to say it back in the passive voice. This can encourage collaboration across the class as they contribute their ideas. The passive is not common in speech so there are often some interesting suggestions.
● **Odd texts:** Invite the children to write texts that would normally be written in the active voice in the passive voice instead. They could try a letter to a friend or an explanation of how a problem occurred in the playground. Ask them to consider how it changes the tone.

Digital content

On the digital component you will find:
● Printable versions of all three photocopiable pages.
● Answers to 'Transforming sentences' and 'Sentence switching'.
● Interactive version of 'Transforming sentences'.

Forming the passive

Transforming sentences

Sentences can be changed from the active voice to the passive voice.

| Gran broke the plate. | The plate was broken by Gran. |

This usually involves
the subject (who does the verb) moving to after the verb.

and the object (what or who the verb is acting upon)
moving to before the verb.

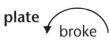

The verb has a word like 'was' or 'were' added and the word 'by' to show who
did the action.

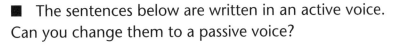

■ The sentences below are written in an active voice.
Can you change them to a passive voice?

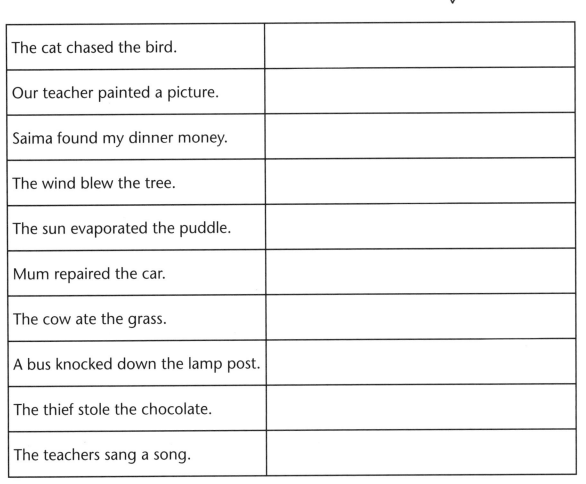

The cat chased the bird.	
Our teacher painted a picture.	
Saima found my dinner money.	
The wind blew the tree.	
The sun evaporated the puddle.	
Mum repaired the car.	
The cow ate the grass.	
A bus knocked down the lamp post.	
The thief stole the chocolate.	
The teachers sang a song.	

Name:

Forming the passive

Changing voices

■ Look through various texts, such as magazines, newspapers, story books or textbooks and find some sentences written in the active voice. Add the sentences to the table. Can you rewrite them in the passive voice?

Sentence in active voice	Rewritten in passive voice

PHOTOCOPIABLE

Forming the passive

Sentence switching

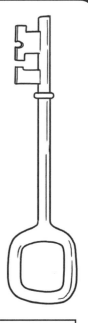

■ Look at the clauses in the table below.

Active voice	Passive voice
I hid the key.	The key was hidden by me.

■ Where the clause is in the active voice, write it in the passive voice.
■ Where the clause is in the passive voice, write it in the active voice.

Active voice	Passive voice
The pirates drew the map.	
	The treasure was buried by pirates.
	The map was stolen by a thief.
The thief lost the map.	
We found the map.	
	The map was followed by us.
We found the treasure.	
The museum looked after the treasure.	

Relative clauses

Objective

Use relative clauses beginning with 'who', 'which', 'where', 'when', 'whose', 'that' or with an implied (omitted) relative pronoun.

Background knowledge

A main clause is a type of independent clause. Main clauses are able to stand alone and present a complete thought, for example: *I have had a quotation*. Subordinate clauses, also known as dependent clauses, are joined to main clauses. They tell us more about the main clauses. They have a subject and a verb, but cannot stand alone as complete sentences because they do not present a complete thought, for example: *for a builder to extend my house*.

A relative clause is a type of subordinate clause that modifies a noun. It often does this by using a relative pronoun, such as 'who' or 'that', to refer back to that noun (though the relative pronoun 'that' is often omitted).

Clauses are useful for improving the quality of writing. A simple sentence only has a main clause. A compound sentence, as the name implies, has more parts. It contains two independent clauses that are linked either by coordinating conjunctions ('and', 'but', 'for', 'or', 'so', 'yet'), a conjunctive adverb ('then', 'almost', 'otherwise'), a semicolon or dash. Complex sentences have a main clause linked to a dependent clause.

Activities

● **Photocopiable page 71 'The cause of the clause'**
This activity reinforces the work on the subjects of verbs. The children are then asked to identify main clauses, relative clauses and other types of dependent clauses.

● **Photocopiable page 72 'Find a clause'**
This activity develops the children's understanding of clauses. It is important to stress that relative clauses are just one type of subordinate clause. The children need to understand this in order to be able to answer the final question. The four subordinate clauses are all relative clauses because they increase our knowledge of a noun in the main clause.

● **Photocopiable page 73 'Add a clause'**
This activity links the work done on the active and passive voices with that done on clauses. The children are given examples of main clauses in the passive or active voice and have to add relative and other types of subordinate clauses to them.

Further ideas

● **Relative clause challenge:** Ask the children to make up main clauses in pairs. They should then share these with another pair and challenge them to extend the sentence using a relative clause.

● **Tell it as it is:** Ask the children to work in groups to prepare a presentation on clauses for Year 5 children. This should include definitions of main and subordinate clauses, explanations of their use and examples.

● **Find out for yourselves:** Ask the children to use the internet to research which subordinating conjunctions and relative pronouns can link clauses together.

● **Show them how it's done:** Use the results of 'Find out for yourselves' (above) to make a class display. Display the children's lists and ask the children to write examples on the display.

Digital content

On the digital component you will find:
● Printable versions of all three photocopiable pages.
● Answers to 'The cause of the clause' and 'Find a clause'.
● Interactive version of 'Find a clause'.

Relative clauses

The cause of the clause

Clauses are useful for improving your writing. All sentences have a main clause, which contains a subject and a verb.

■ Circle the subject in the following sentences.

1. I am arriving at noon.

2. Tomorrow will be cold.

3. English is a wonderful subject.

The sentences below all have two clauses. One is the main clause, the other is a type of subordinate clause called a relative clause. Relative clauses tell us more about the noun in the main clause.

■ Underline the main clauses and circle the relative clauses in these sentences.

4. I bought some sweets that tasted very bitter.

5. I bowled to Ravid who then hit the ball through a window.

6. I went to New York, which is in America.

7. I play football, which I really enjoy.

8. I went to see Davina, who is a friend of mine.

The sentences below also contain subordinate clauses, but they are not relative clauses as they do not give us more information about the noun.

■ Circle the subordinate clauses.

9. We scored three goals before half-time.

10. Cher stayed in the cottage until the evening.

11. On holiday I swam after breakfast.

SCHOLASTIC
www.scholastic.co.uk   **PHOTOCOPIABLE**   **Scholastic English Skills**
Grammar and punctuation: Year 6   71

Name:

Relative clauses

Find a clause

■ Circle the main clauses in the sentences below.

1. I wanted to go to the park but it was raining.

2. Today was a good day.

3. Winning an Olympic gold medal is an achievement that cannot be equalled.

4. She ran the 100 metres in 14 seconds, which was pretty good for her age.

■ Circle the subordinate clauses in the sentences below.

5. I will go to the match if I can get a ticket.

6. The weather tomorrow will be warm yet still rainy.

7. I am going to buy some shoes after school.

8. I like maths although I am not very good at it.

9. I was offered a job that I turned down.

■ Circle the conjunctions that link the clauses in the sentences below.

10. Ed didn't like the look of the spider that was hiding in the bath.

11. Ellie left Rosie who stayed a little longer.

12. We went to the market where we bought some tomatoes.

13. She was the girl who I knew most well.

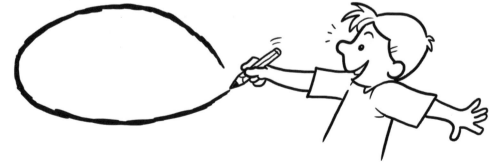

■ What type of subordinate clause are in sentences 10–13?

_____

Relative clauses

Add a clause

All of the sentences below can be extended by adding a subordinate clause.

■ The following sentences all use the active voice. Extend them by adding a relative clause.

1. Jamie passed the ball to Jude

_____

2. Connie watched the seagull

_____

3. Igor led the visitors towards the castle

_____

4. Jemal showed me a picture of his uncle

_____

5. I went to Paris

_____

■ The following sentences all use the passive voice. Extend them by adding a subordinate clause.

6. An apology was offered

_____

7. Two points were scored

_____

8. Refugees were transported to safety

_____

9. Dogs were banned from the beach

_____

10. Our car was stolen

_____

Writing in the active and passive voice

Objective

Write sentences and texts in both the active and passive voice.

Writing focus

Building on previous activities, this section encourages children to use and apply their knowledge of the active and passive voice in their writing, reframing sentences and finding out where and when they can switch from active to passive.

Skills to writing

● It weren't me

The way to get used to the passive voice is to try it out. Encourage children to try rewording sentences and the idea will catch on. Suggest that using the passive voice can be a way of passing on bad news without accepting or laying blame. For example, *while you were out a vase was broken* sounds better than *I broke a vase while you were out*. Give the children a range of sentences to rewrite, removing the 'blame'.

● Who did what?

Ask the children to work in pairs to write a script for a conversation between a parent and their child. The parent asks questions, keen to know what the child has done at school, but the child doesn't want to give too much away, so must always answer in the passive. For example: *"What happened at school today?" "Our class was taught by a new teacher."*

● The subject

When looking at sentences, sharing writing or constructing a text, ask the children to keep an eye out for the subject in a sentence. This means looking at the verb and asking who the subject of the verb is. In active sentences, the subject will do the action of the verb, such as: *Alex broke the window*. 'Alex' is the subject because he broke the window. Make the subject a focus for reflection when the children are writing in the passive voice. In a passive sentence, the action of the verb is done to the subject, such as: *The window was broken by Alex.* In this sentence the subject is the 'window' and 'by Alex' is a preposition phrase. The subject is what the sentence is all about so have they used the best noun. Have they been specific enough? *The being ran up the steps* isn't the same as *The vampire ran up the steps*. Encourage the children to qualify the subject with additional description.

● Hide the object

Ask the children to work in pairs to write five sentences in which the sentences are active and the object is implied. The children should then swap their sentences with another pair of children who try to work out what the actual objects of the sentences would be.

Activities

● Photocopiable page 76 "'Was' and 'by' sentences'

The 'was' and 'by' examples and model sentences provide a way for children to attempt to produce their own examples of passive sentences. They will need to identify a verb that can fit in the middle space and participants either side. Asking them to begin with some interesting verbs, or giving possible verbs they could use, provides a way of getting the activity started.

● Photocopiable page 77 'Passive diary challenge'

The passive diary challenge involves children in an extreme use of the passive voice. It is not the natural mode of diary writing so the exercise leads to oddities of language and presents quite a challenge. Some children may need to list the events of their day first and possibly even write it out in the active voice before they can change it into the passive.

Write on

● A passive speech

Challenge the children to write a speech on a subject of their choice. It could be a football match, a visit they have been on or a favourite activity. Add in the extra condition that they need to try to make the speech in the passive voice.

● Excuses script

Children can try writing a short sketch in which a child is alerting an adult to some awful thing that they have done. Can they wrap the 'crime' up in passive sentences that include only verbs and subjects and so try to make it all sound better? What will the adult ask to tease out the truth?

● Subject in story

Ask the children to plan five paragraphs for a story. Each paragraph should have an action taking place within it. Ask them to look at the actions and ask who the subject is. Can they make their story a bit more interesting by changing the subject and adding in a character? They should avoid adding too many as this can lead to confusion, but encourage them to add in a different character to perform an action. If, for example, their character saves himself from drowning in a torrent, could they alter the story, handing this activity to a new character who becomes the hero? They could then build this character in throughout the story.

● Whodunnits

Picking up on the idea of the subject doing the verb, this could be a good time to ask the children to try plotting out a 'whodunnit'. A crime is committed and clues are left as to 'whodunnit', but their story also needs a few other characters who could have done it. Each of these should do something to make them suspicious. One variation on this is to make the 'whodunnit' the theft of a giant chocolate bar from the teacher's desk, and then to set the scene with all its clues throughout the school.

● The book club

Tell the children that the following books are all available in the school's book club:
- Letters and Parcels Delivered by the Postman
- Speeding Drivers Caught by the Police Officer
- Photographs Taken by Lord Lichfield
- The Battle of Hastings won by William the Conqueror

Ask the children to rewrite the titles in both the active and passive voices.

Digital content

On the digital component you will find:
- Printable versions of both photocopiable pages.

Name:

'Was' and 'by' sentences

■ Look at these sentences. In each of them **something was done by someone
or something**.

Chloe _____ was _____ scared _____ by _____ the frightening mask.

The farmer _____ was _____ chased _____ by _____ the bull.

The earth _____ was _____ saved _____ by _____ Superwoman.

■ Insert subjects, verbs and prepositional phrases into the spaces below to
make your own 'was' and 'by' sentences.

subject	verb	prepositional phrase
	was	by
	was	by
	was	by
	was	by
	was	by
	was	by

■SCHOLASTIC
www.scholastic.co.uk

Writing in the active and passive voice

Passive diary challenge

When we write a diary we say what we did.

It is a challenge to try writing one in the passive voice.

Dear Diary
Today I made my breakfast and caught the bus to school. I played football. We did our maths then we watched a television programme…

Dear Diary
My breakfast was made by me and the bus was caught to school. Football was played and maths was done. A television programme was watched…

■ Write a diary entry in the passive voice. Try to vary your sentences by including some that only have a subject and a verb. For example: *A television programme was watched.*

Dear Diary

_____   _____

_____   _____

_____   _____

_____   _____

_____   _____

_____   _____

_____   _____

_____   _____

SCHOLASTIC
www.scholastic.co.uk   PHOTOCOPIABLE   **Scholastic English Skills**
Grammar and punctuation: Year 6   77

Chapter 4

Cohesion, organisation and presentation

Introduction

This chapter builds on the work done in Year 5. The early parts of this chapter cover cohesive devices. Later parts deal with layout and organisational devices that help to structure the children's writing. For further practice, please see the 'Cohesion, organisation and presentation' section of the Year 6 workbook.

In this chapter

Linking ideas across paragraphs page 81	Link ideas across paragraphs using cohesive devices.
Writing cohesively page 85	Use a wide range of cohesive devices effectively.
Presenting writing page 89	Use organisational and presentational devices to structure text.
Guiding the reader page 93	Use layout devices to structure text and guide the reader.
Organising writing page 97	Write cohesively, considering how to organise and present writing.

Poster notes

Cohesive devices (page 79)

This poster reminds the children of the cohesive devices that they have covered in Year 5. Determiners, conjunctions, adverbs, pronouns, adverbials, synonyms and ellipsis are shown as building blocks that work in conjunction to make writing more cohesive. Use the poster as a starting point to discuss what each type of cohesive device does. The children could work in pairs to give examples for each type.

Give your writing structure (page 80)

This poster shows a range of presentational and structural devices that the children can use to add cohesion to their writing. Paragraphs, titles, text boxes, columns, subheadings, bullet points, bold text and underlining are represented as building blocks to reflect their interlocking nature. Use the poster as a starting point for exploring how each could be used. Lead the children through a discussion of what each device looks like and what it does. Encourage them to find examples of each one from their reading.

Vocabulary

Children should already know:
adverbial, ambiguity, cohesion, determiner, paragraph

In Year 6 children need to know:
bullet point, ellipsis

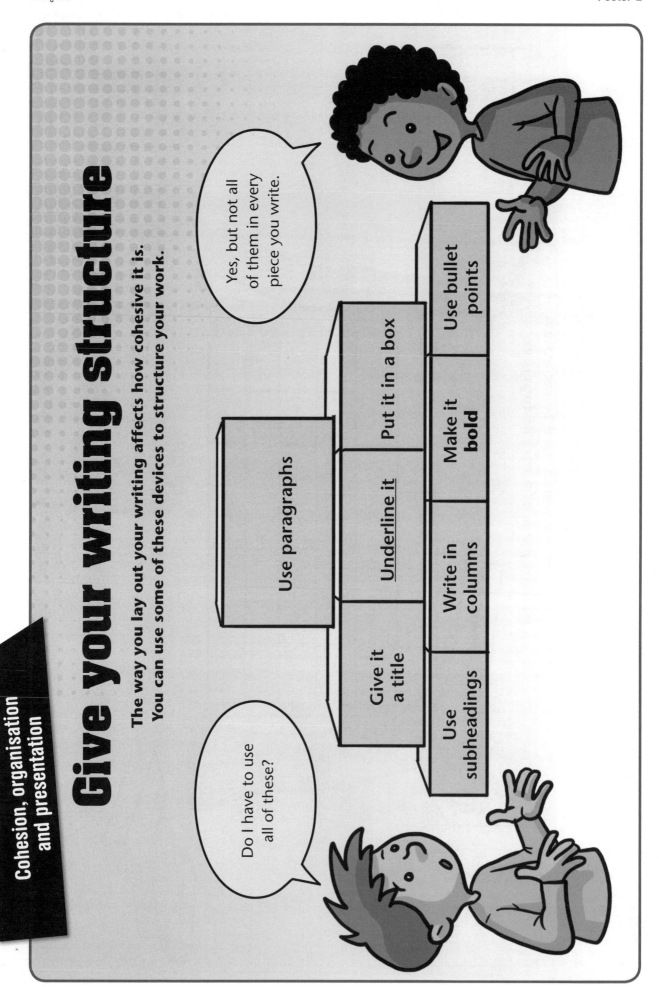

Linking ideas across paragraphs

Objective

Link ideas across paragraphs using cohesive devices.

Background knowledge

The activities in this section build upon the work done in Year 5. It is expected that the children will know about the use of pronouns, adverbs, adverbials of frequency, place, manner and time, conjunctions, synonyms, determiners and ellipsis.

Pronouns replace nouns; adverbs modify verbs, adjectives and even other adverbs; adverbials are similar to adverbs but they have more detail in them; conjunctions link clauses and can be either coordinating or subordinating; synonyms are words that have similar meanings; determiners are placed before nouns and any modifiers; ellipsis can mean the three ellipsis points to show omission but in the Programme of Study it refers specifically to the omission of words that are expected, predictable or superfluous.

The children need to think clearly about what cohesion means and how they can achieve it.

Activities

● **Photocopiable page 82 'The missing link'**
In this activity, the children are asked to identify and match words and phrases with their correct device. Two types of device are omitted. The children will need to identify these and write new labels for them. The missing devices are synonyms and ellipsis.

● **Photocopiable page 83 'Adverbial links across paragraphs'**
The children are presented with three images that represent the action in three consecutive paragraphs of a short story. Invite the children to describe what is happening in each image. Then ask them to link the images by suggesting appropriate adverbials of time, place and frequency.

● **Photocopiable page 84 'Go with the flow'**
The children are given three pieces of writing. Each piece contains the end of one paragraph and the

second sentence of the next paragraph. They have to choose three different types of link and insert them into the appropriate places. They also have to identify the links they have used. This activity will assess their understanding of linking ideas across paragraphs by using cohesive devices.

Further ideas

● **Tennis links:** Give the children a list of the different types of cohesive devices. In pairs, the children take it in turns to 'serve' a cohesive device to their partners. The partner has to give an example of the device, for example: *Adverbial of time – Yesterday morning*. If the partner is correct within ten seconds, they win a point and serve back. The first to five points is the winner.

● **Making links:** This is a continuation game. In groups of four, the children try to continue a story using a range of adverbials. Give the children an opening sentence, such as: *Ida had been waiting for her friend, Rona, for a long time*. Each person in the group continue the story in turn. As they do, they write it down. Allow five minutes and then listen to the new stories. Check with the rest of the class that each group has only used adverbials and count the number they have used.

● **Class display:** On a display board, write down the different types of cohesive devices. Ask the children to add examples of them to the display.

● **It took place then:** Give the children a range of events and times, such as: *Evie went to the market at 12 o'clock*. Ask them to rewrite the statements using adverbials of time, such as 'before'. They are not allowed to use the time from the statement you have given them. For example: *Evie went to the market just before lunch*.

Digital content

On the digital component you will find:
● Printable versions of all three photocopiable pages.
● Answers to 'The missing link'.

Name:

The missing link

Archie is an explorer. He has discovered a group of cohesive devices that he has never seen before. He needs to examine them and put them into categories.

■ Help him by drawing lines to connect the words and phrases with the correct cohesive device.

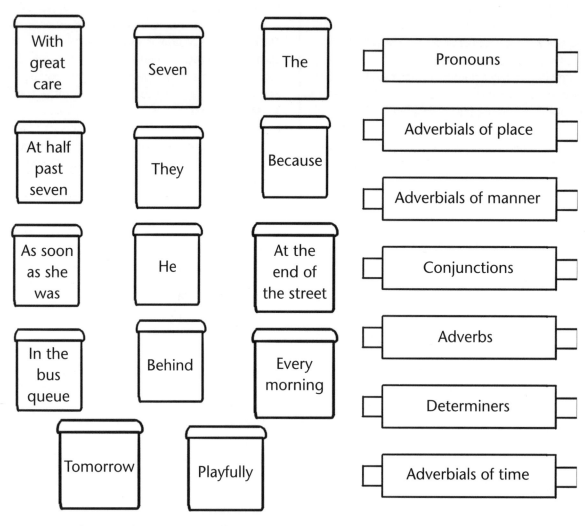

■ Two cohesive devices are still missing. Can you help Archie by writing new labels for them below?

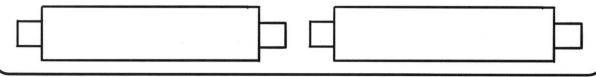

PHOTOCOPIABLE

■ SCHOLASTIC
www.scholastic.co.uk

Linking ideas across paragraphs

Adverbial links across paragraphs

The images below tell a short story. Each image represents one paragraph of the story.

Image 1

Image 2

Image 3

■ In the boxes below, write what you think is happening in each picture.

1.

2.

3.

■ The events in the story need to be linked together so that the paragraphs have cohesion. In the boxes below, write links to begin the paragraphs for images 2 and 3 using the appropriate adverbials. One has been done for you as an example.

	Adverbials of time	Adverbials of place	Adverbials of frequency
Link image 1 to 2	*Some time later, the bus arrived.*		
Link image 2 to 3			

■SCHOLASTIC
www.scholastic.co.uk   **PHOTOCOPIABLE**   **Scholastic English Skills**
Grammar and punctuation: Year 6   **83**

Name:

Go with the flow

We can use a range of cohesive devices to make sure our writing flows from one paragraph to the next.

■ Each piece of writing below contains the end of one paragraph and the second sentence of the next paragraph. Use a cohesive device to write the missing sentence.

■ Write the name of each cohesive device you have used in the boxes. You can only use each device once.

1. Bernie watched as the ship set sail, leaving him behind.

_____

He knew he would be on the island for a long, long time.

Cohesive device: [   ]

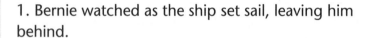

2. There was nothing more Bernie could do.

_____

Bernie sat down, realising that there was nothing he could do.

Cohesive device: [   ]

3. He couldn't believe his eyes. The ship was coming back!

_____

He ran into the water and grabbed at the rope that was being offered to him.

Cohesive device: [   ]

Writing cohesively

Objective

Use a wide range of cohesive devices effectively.

Background knowledge

The focus of this section is on developing the children's ability to use a range of cohesive devices. The children will know about the use of pronouns, adverbs, adverbials of frequency, place, manner and time, conjunctions, synonyms and determiners. Previously, they have used them individually. For this section, they will need to use them together.

Ellipsis is considered separately. Ensure the children are aware that ellipsis is not limited to the punctuation mark (…). Ellipsis comes from the Greek *elleipein*, meaning to leave out. Therefore, in its true form, ellipsis is when words or phrases are left out by the writer but the reader is still able to understand the meaning using contextual clues. The words that are omitted are expected or predictable but they are also superfluous. For example, in the sentence *She did it because she wanted to*, two words are omitted at the end. The full sentence would be *She did it because she wanted to do it*, but the ending is obvious so it is missed out. The ellipsis points (…) are punctuation marks that can be used to denote where ellipsis has taken place.

Activities

● **Photocopiable page 86 'Link it up'**
Invite the children to complete three paragraphs by inserting different cohesive devices into them. The devices will fit in more than one place so the children have to pick the ones that will make the most sense.

● **Photocopiable page 87 'What's not needed?'**
In this activity, the children use their understanding of ellipsis to remove superfluous words and phrases. They also need to use synonyms (in this case pronouns such as 'he', 'she', 'they' and 'it') to avoid repeating the same word or phrase.

● **Photocopiable page 88 'Ellipsis'**
The children are given a set of replies to questions and have to work out which words could be missed out (elided). They then focus on sentences that have already been elided and try to work out which (predictable) words are missing.

Further ideas

● **Superfluous:** In pairs, ask each child to write a sentence including a superfluous word or phrase. The children swap sentences and try to correct them by identifying the superfluous parts and, if necessary, rewriting them.

● **Join me:** Give the children a number of adverbials of time, place, or manner. Ask them to use some of these to write a paragraph about an event of their choice.

● **Join us:** Using the paragraphs the children have written for 'Join me', ask them to share their work with a partner. The partner then has to change the piece by adding conjunctions to link some of the sentences. Finally, the pair should check that they have no unnecessary words or phrases and edit them if necessary.

● **How long can you make it?:** Challenge the children to write the longest sentence they can without using superfluous or repeated words. Ask the children to swap their sentences with a partner. The partner should check to ensure that there is nothing in the sentences that could be omitted. Display the longest sentences around the classroom walls.

Digital content

On the digital component you will find:
● Printable versions of all three photocopiable pages.
● Answers to 'What's not needed?' and 'Ellipsis'.
● Interactive versions of 'Link it up' and 'What's not needed?'.

Name:

Writing cohesively

Link it up

Zoe has invented a paragraph machine. Unfortunately, it is not working properly. It is missing out cohesive devices. She needs to use some words from her device boxes to complete the paragraphs.

■ Help Zoe to complete the paragraphs by choosing appropriate words or phrases from the boxes. You need to use three different devices in each paragraph and you cannot use the same words or phrases twice.

Adverbials of time	Adverbials of place
last week a few days ago a little later some time afterwards	behind the dresses above the door in front

Determiners	Conjunctions
seven more the some all few her	but yet because for and so

_____ my sister went to the shops in the city centre. She had

plenty of money _____ she couldn't see anything she wanted

to buy. Just when she thought that she would come home empty handed, she

went into a shop and saw _____ dresses that she liked.

_____ was another rack of trousers. My sister looked closely at

_____ of them but she didn't buy any _____

she had run out of money.

A sign _____ told my sister that the shop closed soon. She

looked at her watch and saw that she had only _____ minutes

to catch the bus home. She ran to the bus stop _____ was too

late and had to get the next one.

Writing cohesively

What's not needed?

When we are writing, we often don't include some words or phrases because the reader can work them out from the rest of the sentence.

■ In the sentences below, underline the words that are not needed and could be missed out.

1. We went on holiday to Ibiza even though my mum didn't want to go there.

2. At the end of the race, her head, her heart and her lungs all ached.

3. At the shop I bought some jeans, some tops and some shoes.

4. You can go to the cinema if you want to go to the cinema.

5. Ronnie watched the end of the television programme and then he went to bed.

To avoid repeating ourselves, we often use pronouns to replace words.

■ In the sentences below, underline the words that have been repeated and then rewrite the sentences using pronouns instead. The first one has been done for you.

6. Jed got a computer for his birthday. He uses his <u>computer</u> to send emails.

Jed got a computer for his birthday. He uses it to send emails.

7. Jennifer and Eva like dancing. Jennifer and Eva go to the dance club every Saturday.

8. Joey is good at chess. Joey plays chess after school.

9. My auntie has a little dog. My auntie's dog is brown and white. My auntie's dog is very friendly.

SCHOLASTIC
www.scholastic.co.uk   **PHOTOCOPIABLE**   Scholastic English Skills
Grammar and punctuation: Year 6   87

Name:

Writing cohesively

Ellipsis

Ellipsis is when expected or predictable words are missed out.

■ In the replies to the questions below, underline the words that are not needed and could be missed out.

1. "Do you want to go to the cinema?"

"No we don't."

2. "Who broke the window?"

"It was me."

3. "Menorca is lovely, isn't it?"

"Yes, it is."

4. "What are you doing?"

"I am playing on my games console."

5. "Who was the mother of Elizabeth I?"

"The mother of Elizabeth I was Anne Boleyn."

■ Try to work out what words have been missed out of the following sentences and write them in the gaps. Remember, they should be predictable.

6. "My brother likes chilli but I don't _____."

7. "Have you met the new maths teacher?" "No _____."

8. "Where did you go on holiday last year?"

"_____ to Florida."

9. "Does your dad always do the ironing in your house?"

"Yes _____."

10. "Who is the faster runner, you or your sister?"

"_____ my sister."

Presenting writing

Objective

Use organisational and presentational devices to structure text.

Background knowledge

The children should already know about some layout and presentational devices, such as headings, subheadings and bullet points. This section will concentrate on using them to help their writing be more cohesive. Headings are used to attract readers by giving them a taste of the overall piece of writing. Subheadings are used to summarise the contents of paragraphs. Both headings and subheadings should be short.

Bullet points are used to organise information concisely into lists. In contrast to numbered lists, bullet points do not necessarily imply an order of importance. The sentence preceding the bullet points should end with a colon. There are a variety of ways to punctuate bullet points but the important thing is to be consistent. If you are listing complete sentences, start each point with a capital letter and end with a full stop. Alternatively, if your list is a continuation of your initial sentence, use lower case and only put a full stop at the end of the final point.

Activities

● **Photocopiable page 90 'Headings'**
The children are given three lists summarising the contents of different news articles. Ask the children to use the information to write short, snappy headings for each article. (You could use this exercise as an introduction to the use of bullet points as well.)

● **Photocopiable page 91 'Headings and subheadings'**
The children are given a complete article about a new sports car. It is split up into sections. Ask the children to read the article and provide an appropriate heading and subheadings.

● **Photocopiable page 92 'Bullet points'**
The children are given three paragraph descriptions of fictitious products. Invite them to break the descriptions down into their most important features, and then rewrite these as bullet point lists.

Further ideas

● **What's the heading?:** Cut out some articles from newspapers and magazines. Give them to the children but cut the headings off first. Ask the children to come up with headings and explain their reasoning for them.

● **Put it all together:** Cut articles from a newspaper or magazine into separate paragraphs. Make sure you do not include any subheadings. Divide the children into groups and give them the paragraphs. Ask the children to rearrange the paragraphs into what they think is the correct order and to write subheadings for each one. You can differentiate this activity by giving more advanced texts to the more confident learners.

● **Bullet point it:** In pairs, ask the children to invent a new product and write a prose summary of its most important features. They then need to create a flyer for the product using bullet points to summarise the details. Display the flyers in the classroom.

● **Today:** Ask the children to make a bullet point list of six things they have done since they got up. This should be very simple and only include statements such as: *I went downstairs*. Encourage the children to add further detail to each bullet point in the form of adverbs and adverbials. The children then have to write a diary entry including all of the information contained in the bullet points and the additional details. The entry must include a heading and subheadings.

Digital content

On the digital component you will find:
● Printable versions of all three photocopiable pages.
● Answers to 'Bullet points'.

Name:

Presenting writing

Headings

KEEP THEM SHORT AND SNAPPY !

The information in each box below lists the content of three different news articles.

■ Write a heading for each article, based on the summary.

1. **Heading:**

- A woman has been caught shoplifting.
- She stole five cans of cat food.
- She was caught as she left the store.
- She is 78 years old.
- She is due in court next week.

NEWSPAPER
BOY BAND CONQUERS CHARTS

2. **Heading:**

- A girl has invented a new app.
- She has sold it to a large software manufacturer.
- She invented it as part of her GCSE course.
- She is 16 years old.
- She intends to stay on at school.

3. **Heading:**

- A man has walked into a police station.
- He does not know who he is.
- He has a membership card for a snooker club in his pocket.
- His age is not known.
- He can quote all of *Romeo and Juliet*.

NEWSPAPER
GIRLS HIT THE HEIGHTS

SCHOLASTIC
www.scholastic.co.uk

Presenting writing

Headings and subheadings

- Read this article about a new sports car.
- Write an appropriate heading for the article and subheadings for each paragraph.

Heading: _____

British sports car manufacturers, Arrowhead, have announced plans for their latest flagship vehicle, the Slingshot.

Subheading: _____

Needing to fight back against strong competition from abroad, having watched their share of the market fall significantly over the last three years, Arrowhead had to do something.

Subheading: _____

Boy have they done it! The Slingshot is a sophisticated product that bears all the hallmarks of its pedigree. Arrowhead is back up there with the best!

Subheading: _____

Managing Director Cerise Brown said, "This is a great achievement. We have gone from the first idea to the production car in less than a year." She continued, "Lots of people will love this car. It goes like a rocket and is very reasonably priced. It's a lot of car for the money."

Subheading: _____

Arrowhead expect to sell 2000 cars this year, each costing over £35,000. A new, top of the range model will be available next year for £47,000. Keep looking in your rear-view mirror, as it will soon be in it!

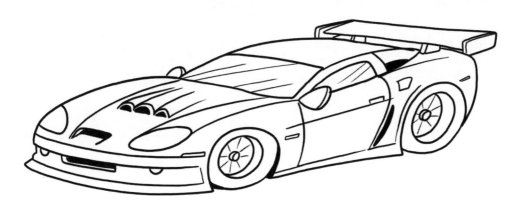

Name:

Presenting writing

Bullet points

■ Read the information about the three products below.
■ Make a bullet point list of the important features of each product.

Fun-Go-Pro

A bright and stylish cycle helmet which is sturdy, safe and affordable. It has ten fun and funky designs to choose from and can be bought in all good bike stores.

Fun-Go-Pro:

● _____

● _____

● _____

● _____

Rabbit Monthly

The complete guide to rabbits and their care. It has a special focus each month – this month looks at how to build your own rabbit hutch. It's a bargain at only £2 per month. It is available from all good newsagents.

Rabbit Monthly:

● _____

● _____

● _____

● _____

Indigo's Invisible Ink

This remarkable product is a new twist on an age old idea. The difference is, Indigo Invisible Ink really works. Used by real spies, this ink is very reliable. Fool your friends and your teachers! It is only available from indigoinvisible@ink.com

Indigo's Invisible Ink:

● _____

● _____

● _____

● _____

Guiding the reader

Objective

Use layout devices to structure text and guide the reader.

Background knowledge

The children will need to be introduced to the use of other layout devices such as columns and tables. Columns and tables are regularly used in newspapers and magazines. They feature more in factual writing than in fiction. Columns are used to make the text easier to read and to help organise it. They break up pages into manageable sections of text that are not off-putting to read. Columns allow editors to put different stories next to each other. Not all columns are of equal length or width. This enables the editor to make the article fit and allows for the inclusion of pictures, tables and advertisements. Tables are used to provide succinct information in a small space. Sometimes tables are used in the body of articles to support the points. They may contain information on only one subject but often they are used for comparisons. Tables often need further explanation in the main text to ensure that the reader interprets them the way they were intended.

Activities

● **Photocopiable page 94 'Laying it out'**
This activity requires the children to design an information leaflet about Siberian tigers using columns, pictures and headings. Do some preliminary work as a class, encouraging the children to examine a range of magazines or newspapers. The children could start by making a bullet point list of the information and using this to decide upon the number of columns, tables and pictures they will use.

● **Photocopiable page 95 'Tables'**
This activity presents the children with information in different formats. They need to restructure the information into three tables of increasing complexity. The activity also revisits the work done on adverbials.

● **Photocopiable page 96 'The front page'**
The children are given elements of the front page of a newspaper. They have to rearrange them to form a typical newspaper layout. They then have to write an explanation for their arrangements.

Further ideas

● **Which would you use?:** Ask the children to research a subject of their own choice and to make a list of five pieces of information about it. Then ask them which presentational device they would use to present the information. They do not actually have to make the presentation but they need to be able to justify their decisions.

● **Sports day:** When sports day is approaching, ask the children to make a table to show the names of the events, the times and the competitors.

● **All about us:** Ask the children to make a class display about themselves. They will each need to write a short autobiographical column. They could interview each other to find information about their hobbies, what books they read, the television programmes they watch, the games they play or the pets they have. This information could be made into tables as part of the display.

● **Anything else?:** We tend to think that magazines are only written in columns. Give the children pages from magazines and ask them to look for other presentational devices such as text boxes, callouts, pull quotes and infographics. Ask them which they think is the most effective at passing information and why.

Digital content

On the digital component you will find:
● Printable versions of all three photocopiable pages.
● Answers to 'Tables'.

Name:

Laying it out

You have been asked to design an information poster about Siberian tigers.

■ Read the following passage.

> Siberian tigers are almost amber in colour, with black stripes. These large animals grow to over 150cm in length and 115cm in height. They can weigh as much as 400kg. These tigers are found in the far east of Russia. Their numbers have been rapidly decreasing. In 2005 there were less than 400 left. They eat deer, bears, rabbits and salmon. The Russian and Chinese governments have agreed to try to protect the tigers to make sure that they do not become extinct. It appears that these efforts are beginning to succeed but much more needs to be done.

■ Use this information to make your poster. You need to use headings, columns, pictures and possibly bullet points in your poster. In the space below, draw columns and write the information in them. Remember that your columns do not all have to be the same size, but the page should feel balanced.

Guiding the reader

Tables

■ You have been asked to create tables for three different situations. Read each brief and create a table to show the information in a way that is easy to understand. Use the space below or a separate sheet of paper.

1. Create a table to show the adverbials of time, place and manner.

2. Create a table for your local library to show which non-fiction subjects girls and boys like to read about.

> You have asked everybody in your class and found out that 8 girls like history, 4 like geography and 3 like science. You have also discovered that 10 boys like sport, 2 like geography, 2 like travel and 1 likes history.

3. Create a table for a car magazine article to compare the features of three family cars.

> The Seddon Sedan has five seats, air conditioning, a satellite navigation system and a CD player. It costs £18,000.
> The Boston Boxer has four seats, air conditioning, a satellite navigation system, but no CD player. It costs £19,000.
> The Thomas Topaz has five seats, no air conditioning, no satellite navigation system and no CD player. It costs £11,000.

Name:

The front page

■ Cut out the items below.

■ On another piece of paper, rearrange them to create the layout of the front page for a newspaper.

■ Write a short explanation of why you have arranged them in that way.

✂

| Newspaper name |
| Heading |
| Subheading |

Column	Column	Column	Picture

Organising writing

Objective

Write cohesively, considering how to organise and present writing.

Writing focus

Building on previous activities, this section provides opportunities for children to think about how to organise and present their writing and ensure cohesion within and across paragraphs, all the time considering the impact of their writing on the reader. The children will have to utilise their knowledge of presentational devices, linking them together to produce finished pieces.

Skills to writing

● **Make a flowchart**
A flowchart is an easy way of explaining a process in a diagram. Explain to the children what a flowchart is and how it can be used. Give them the following example of how to write a letter of complaint:

Make a bullet point list of all the things you want to say and the reasons for them.

↓

Organise the list in order, from the strongest to the weakest points.

↓

Put your address and the date on the top right-hand side of the letter.

↓

Start with 'Dear…'

↓

Write one paragraph for each item in your ordered list.

↓

End with 'Yours…'.

Ask the children to work in pairs. They should follow the format of the example to create their own flowchart showing the steps they would take to design a poster like the one on photocopiable page 94 'Laying it out'. This will encourage the children to think logically and to analyse the process.

● **Link it all together**
Working in pairs, the children write presentations to show the rest of the class how to use presentational devices (headings, subheadings, bullet points, tables, columns and pictures). They must include cohesive devices (ellipsis, adverbials, adverbs, conjunctions, synonyms and determiners) in their presentations to structure their talk and to link the ideas together. They could use the experience they have gained from the previous activity ('Make a flowchart') to help them structure the presentation.

● **Make it simple**
Ask the children to make an information sheet for Year 5 children to explain the use of presentational devices. Start by reminding the children of the presentational devices (headings, subheadings, bullet points, tables, columns and pictures). As well as explaining what they are, the children should use all of the presentational devices they have learned about in the layout of the sheet. The children should consider their choice of language and ensure that it is appropriate for the intended audience.

● **On the web**
Encourage the children to examine the use of presentational devices on websites. Ask them to use the internet to research information for this activity. Lead a class discussion on their findings by prompting them to explain the differences and similarities that exist between electronic and paper-based presentations.

Activities

● **Photocopiable page 99 'Definitions and examples'**

The children have to show their knowledge of cohesive devices by matching the definitions to their names. Once they have done this, they will need to demonstrate their understanding by giving examples for each type of device. Remind the children that ellipsis is the omission of obvious or superfluous words. Their example should show a sentence with the word or words included. They should then rewrite the sentence with the omissions made.

● **Photocopiable page 100 'Information leaflet'**

This activity draws together the work done on presentational and layout devices. It contains a number of pieces of information that, when reassembled, will provide all that is necessary to create an information sheet about girls' football. The children will need to add their own subheadings.

Write on

● **Class newspaper**

When an important event is taking place in your school, such as a school trip, work together to create a class newspaper. On an A3 sheet of paper (or bigger), draw outlines for the name of the newspaper, the title of the article, columns and pictures. Then divide the children into groups and allocate them parts of the article to write, including the subheadings. They could do interviews with the children who go on the trip and even some of the people who work at the venue. Encourage the children to take photographs on the day so they can include them, too. This could be done electronically.

● **The formation of information**

Ask the children to bring in information leaflets. The content is not important – they could be holiday attractions (such as theme parks or other places to visit), instruction manuals, advertisements for sales or events that will take place. Ask the children to find and identify the cohesive and presentational devices that are being used. Once they have done this, they could write an analysis of the leaflet to show the devices that are used and how effective the children think they have been.

● **All about our school**

Invite the children to design an information booklet about their school. They will need to decide who it is for and what will go in it. They will then need to research each section before it is written. Finally, they will need to design the layout and ensure that they have used all of the cohesive and presentational devices that they have covered in this chapter.

Digital content

On the digital component you will find:
● Printable versions of both photocopiable pages.
● Answers to 'Definitions and examples'.
● Interactive version of 'Definitions and examples'.

Organising writing

Definitions and examples

■ Connect the cohesive devices to their definitions.

Words that describe a verb.	Words or phrases about time, place or manner.	Words or phrases missed out.

Ellipsis

Adverbials

Adverbs

Conjunctions

Synonyms

Determiners

Words that tell us how many there are.	Words that join sentences.	Words that mean the same.

■ Give an example for each device.

1. **Ellipsis:** _____

2. **Adverbial:** _____

3. **Adverb:** _____

4. **Conjunction:** _____

5. **Synonym:** _____

6. **Determiner:** _____

Name:

Organising writing

Information leaflet

■ Cut out the information below.

■ On another piece of paper, rearrange them to plan the layout for an information leaflet about girls' football. You will need to write your own subheadings.

Reasons to watch ladies football:
■ **You can support your favourite team.**
■ **It's fast**
■ **It's cheap**
■ **It's new**
■ **It's easy to get tickets**
■ **It's exciting**

Girls' football is growing in popularity. Almost all of the major Premier League teams now have ladies' teams too. There is even a national football league for women, called the FA Women's Super League.

	Pld	W	D	L	GF	GA	GD	Pts
England	3	2	1	0	5	2	+3	7
Japan	3	2	0	1	6	3	+3	6
Mexico	3	0	2	1	3	7	−4	2
New Zealand	3	0	1	2	4	6	−2	1

England even has a national ladies team although, unlike the men's team, it is doing quite well at the moment. In the 2011 World Cup, England won their group but lost 4–1 to France in the knockout round that followed.

Some of the women are full-time professional players and earn their living playing the game. They don't get paid anything like their male counterparts though. Perhaps they should.

At the moment there are no plans for England to bid for the Women's World Cup in 2019.

You can find out more about girls' football at www.thefa.com/womens-girls-football

IT'S A GIRLS' GAME TOO

PHOTOCOPIABLE

SCHOLASTIC
www.scholastic.co.uk

Chapter 5

Punctuation

Introduction

Punctuation is a vital part of writing. It structures the writing, makes it cohesive and helps us to read and understand it. It tells us when to pause and how long for. It shows us who is speaking. It can even tell us how something should sound. In this chapter, the children will be introduced to semicolons, colons and dashes (hyphens). They will revisit brackets (parentheses) and inverted commas (speech marks). Finally, they will attempt to use the new punctuation marks in their own writing. For further practice, please see the 'Punctuation' section of the Year 6 workbook.

In this chapter

Colons, semicolons and dashes page 104	Use a colon to introduce a list and semicolons within lists.
Separating clauses page 108	Use colons, semicolons and dashes to mark the boundary between independent clauses.
Hyphens page 112	Understand how hyphens can be used.
Using punctuation page 116	Apply knowledge of punctuation.
Punctuation in writing page 120	Secure the use of a wide range of punctuation in writing.

Poster notes

Colons, semicolons and dashes (page 102)
Unlike some punctuation marks, colons, semicolons and dashes all have multiple uses. Children often find this confusing and treat them as though they are interchangeable. This poster outlines their uses and gives practical examples of each. Use the examples to draw the children's attention to their differences.

Mark the punctuation (page 103)
This poster is a summary of the punctuation marks that the children will already know. Ask the children what the function of each mark is and then ask them to find examples of it in the text. Remind the children that ellipsis is not just the symbol, but describes the omission of repeated, predictable or superfluous words. Also, ensure that the children understand the difference between parenthesis (brackets) and the concept of parenthesis, which describes the insertion of a clause or phrase into a sentence that provides additional detail.

Vocabulary

Children should already know:
apostrophe, bracket, comma, dash, exclamation mark, full stop, inverted comma, parenthesis, question mark, speech mark
In Year 6 children need to know:
colon, hyphen, semicolon

Punctuation

Colons, semicolons and dashes

Colons	Semicolons	Dashes
To introduce lists For this drink you need: four oranges, two lemons, some lemonade.	**To mark the boundary between two independent clauses** The water evaporated; I said it would.	**To show a change of thought (like ellipses)** "You are my friend….my best friend." "You are my friend – my best friend."
To introduce summaries We have learned the following: sugar dissolves in tea.	**To show a link between two things** Salt dissolves; sugar does too.	**To mark the boundary between two independent clauses** The water evaporated – I said it would.
To introduce examples Some materials dissolve, for example: salt in water; sugar in coffee.	**To separate complicated items within a list** The three dishes contained: salt and sugar; salt and water; salt on its own.	**To show something is following (like colons)** Some materials dissolve, for example: salt in water; sugar in coffee. Some materials dissolve – salt in water; sugar in coffee.
To introduce quotations My teacher says: "The colon is really useful."	**Semicolons are stronger than commas, but weaker than full stops.**	**Dashes are used more informally than other punctuation marks.**
To mark the boundary between two independent clauses The water evaporated: it turned into water vapour.		

PHOTOCOPIABLE

SCHOLASTIC
www.scholastic.co.uk

Punctuation

Mark the punctuation

Can you find all of the punctuation in this passage?

Are you looking for punctuation marks? You've come to the right place! My teacher says, "Start with a full stop." (Isn't that wrong? You end with a full stop…don't you?) I'm good at punctuation but my brother, Jack, isn't. Jack's work is full of mistakes, crossings out and corrections. I'm sure he could do better if only…

question mark

exclamation mark

comma

ellipsis

speech marks

full stop

brackets

It's apostrophe of contraction

's apostrophe of possession

Colons, semicolons and dashes

Objective

Use a colon to introduce a list and semicolons within lists.

Background knowledge

The primary focus of this section is on using colons, semicolons and dashes in lists. However, it is useful to be aware of their other uses.

Colons are used to introduce lists; introduce summaries; introduce examples; introduce quotations; introduce second clauses that expand or illustrate the first; separate one clause from another: without separating them completely (as with a full stop).

Semicolons can mark the boundary between two independent clauses; show a link between two things; separate complicated items within in a list. Semicolons are stronger than commas, but weaker than full stops.

Dashes can show a change of thought (like ellipses); mark the boundary between two independent clauses (like semicolons); show something is following (like colons). Dashes are used more informally than other punctuation marks.

Activities

● **Photocopiable page 105 'Using colons to introduce lists'**
This sheet tests the children's understanding of the use of colons by asking them to list the possibilities. It then asks them to reorganise the list into bullet points introduced by a colon. Finally, the children are given a list without punctuation and are asked to rewrite it using a colon and commas.

● **Photocopiable page 106 'Using semicolons within a list'**
The children are asked to rewrite two shopping lists. This activity revisits the use of commas in lists but then moves on to semicolons and builds on the work done on using colons in lists. Remind the children that they need to include a colon at the start of each list.

● **Photocopiable page 107 'Colons and semicolons in lists'**
The children are invited to arrange the text into an appropriate order and separate it using the correct punctuation. They then have to explain the reasoning behind their choices. They may well have the texts in a variety of orders. Ask the children why, although there are numerous ways to organise the texts, there is only one correct way to organise the punctuation.

Further ideas

● **Quotes book:** Ask the children to include colons when recording quotations in a 'quotes book'. They can staple some pages of A5 paper together and, over time, record the words members of their family or people in their neighbourhood are renowned for saying.
● **The long list:** Make a display on the wall that starts with *I went to the shop and I bought:* Each day a different child should add a new item and a semicolon to extend the list. Challenge them to add items in alphabetical order until the last child finishes the list with a full stop.
● **We'd like to…:** Ask the children to think of what they would like to do before they leave the school and to present their ideas as bullet point lists and lists in continuous prose. Display the lists on the classroom wall and ask the children to tick them off as they complete them.

Digital content

On the digital component you will find:
● Printable versions of all three photocopiable pages.
● Answers for all three photocopiable pages.

Colons, semicolons and dashes

Using colons to introduce lists

■ List the main uses of colons.

1. _____

2. _____

3. _____

4. _____

5. _____

■ Rewrite your list in bullet points starting with 'The main uses of colons are' followed by the correct punctuation.

_____

• _____

• _____

• _____

• _____

• _____

■ Rewrite the following list using a colon and commas.
I went to the shops and I bought an apple a banana a corkscrew and a doormat.

_____

_____

Use a colon to introduce a list.

Name:

Using semicolons within a list

some potatoes

some rice

a jar of Madras curry paste

some onions

some peppers

some garlic

■ Punctuate the shopping list using a colon to introduce it and commas to separate the items.

My mother asked me to bring home_____

_____

_____

_____

Sometimes, lists have more details in them and commas are not strong enough to separate them so we use semicolons.

2kg potatoes from the market

5kg rice and a jar of Madras curry paste from Patel's

1kg of Spanish onions and a mixture of red, green and yellow peppers from Murphy's minimart

a large garlic bulb from the grocer's

■ Punctuate this shopping list using a colon to introduce it and semicolons to separate the items.

My father asked me to bring home_____

_____

_____

_____

PHOTOCOPIABLE ■SCHOLASTIC
www.scholastic.co.uk

Colons, semicolons and dashes

Colons and semicolons in lists

- ■ Cut out all of the punctuation marks and text below.
- ■ Arrange them all so the text is correctly punctuated.

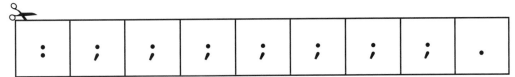

| : | ; | ; | ; | ; | ; | ; | ; | . |

Astrid, the tallest girl in the class
I think the best players for the school netball team are
and Ellie because she shoots really accurately
Rachel, a really good organiser
Carla because she can catch better than anyone
Armani, who never gives the ball away
Luisa because she is very fast
Erin who always defends well

- ■ Explain your choices.

I used the colon because

_____

I used the semicolons because

_____

I used the full stop because

_____

Separating clauses

Objective

Use colons, semicolons and dashes to mark the boundary between independent clauses.

Background knowledge

As well as being used in lists, colons, semicolons and dashes are also used to demarcate sentences. They allow the writer to develop complex sentences without the complication of multiple commas. They are used specifically to mark the boundary between two independent clauses. An independent clause contains at least a verb and a subject and can stand alone as a complete sentence. By using punctuation to separate them we put a clear pause between the first independent clause and the second.

Colons can be used to introduce a second independent clause that amplifies and gives further explanation to a preceding sentence. The colon shows that the second clause has a clear link to the first and is an extension of the train of thought but it gives more emphasis to the second one.

Semicolons can link two related clauses of equal strength. Dashes can be used almost identically to semicolons, but often in less formal writing.

Activities

● **Photocopiable page 109 'Colons and clauses'**
The children are asked to punctuate sentences using colons and to add independent clauses. Ensure they understand that an independent clause can stand alone as a complete sentence. It will have a verb and a subject.
● **Photocopiable page 110 'Semicolons, colons and clauses'**
The children are asked to demarcate independent clauses by inserting colons or semicolons and then explain their choices. Questions 1 and 3 should have semicolons because both clauses have equal weight. Questions 2 and 4 should be colons because the second

clause is more important than the first. Finally, the children have to answer two questions to demonstrate their understanding further.
● **Photocopiable page 111 'Dashes'**
The children have to distinguish between dashes, semicolons and colons in three sentences. The children then have to decide in which sentence dashes are used correctly. The correct answer is number 4 because it is the only one with two independent clauses: *'The film was brilliant'* and *'I went to see it again'*, can both stand alone as independent sentences. They are separated by the dashes and the interjection.

Further ideas

● **Writing type:** Colons, semicolons and dashes all perform particular roles in certain types of writing. For example, they can clarify the explanation of a science task or the listing of items used in a technology project. As these punctuation marks are introduced to the children, look at texts across the curriculum, focusing on writing in which their use could be reinforced. Ask the children to identify which punctuation marks are being used in the texts. Then ask them to explain why they have been chosen in preference to other possible choices.
● **Taking sentences apart:** Provide the children with other texts that they can look at closely to see where colons, semicolons or dashes have been used to demarcate grammatical boundaries. When they have identified the separate parts of a sentence, they should focus on the question: *What distinctive thing does each part say?*
● **Can you use them?:** Ask the children to select a passage from a text they are reading and then to rewrite it as a summary of the events, using colons, semicolons or dashes as appropriate to punctuate their writing.

Digital content

On the digital component you will find:
● Printable versions of all three photocopiable pages.
● Answers for all three photocopiable pages.
● Interactive version of 'Semicolons, colons and clauses'.

Separating clauses

Colons and clauses

■ Put the colon in the correct place in each of these sentences.

1. Ranvir looked at his work he had scored full marks again.

2. Johan readjusted his sights he would need to be more accurate in future.

3. Larissa worked hard it was the only way to earn lots of money.

4. My pet snail pulled his head back into his shell he was not going to come out again today.

■ Add an appropriate independent clause to complete these statements.

5. Odal the Wizard knew what his most important wish would be:

_____

6. Mrs Spikey looked at her new haircut in the mirror:

_____

7. It all rested on one spin of a coin:

_____

8. Hassan the Horrible looked across the battleground:

_____

Separating clauses

Semicolons, colons and clauses

■ Each of the following sentences has a space that should contain a colon or a semicolon to link independent clauses. Write in which one you think it should be.

1. It's Jack's birthday tomorrow ____ Ted's birthday is next week.

2. Exam success is important ____ you have to work hard to achieve it.

3. July was very cold and wet ____ August will be much the same.

4. It's the big match tomorrow ____ we have to win it.

■ Pick two of your answers. Explain why you used a colon in one and a semicolon in the another.

In sentence number _____ I used a colon because.

_____

_____

In sentence number _____ I used a semicolon because

_____

_____

■ What would be the effect of replacing the full stop in the middle of this example with a semicolon?

Jill loved Joe. Joe loved her too.

_____

_____

■ Why is the colon used in the sentence below?

James knew he had to score the penalty: this was the final chance to win the match.

_____

_____

Dashes

■ Make the following sentences correct by putting either dashes, colons or semicolons in the boxes.

1. That car's jamming the road ▢ little can get past.

2. Your car is in the way ▢ it's blocking the road.

3. I watched a scary film last night ▢ it was very frightening.

■ Explain your choices.

In sentence number 1 I used a _____ because

_____

_____

In sentence number 2 I used a _____ because

_____

_____

In sentence number 3 I used a _____ because

_____

_____

■ Which of these sentences is correct? Explain your answer.

4. The film was brilliant – fantastic, in fact – I went to see it again.
5. The film was – brilliant fantastic in fact – so I went to see it again.
6. The film was – brilliant, fantastic, in fact so – I went to see it again.
7. The film was brilliant – fantastic – in fact, so I went to see it again.

Sentence number _____ is correct because

_____

_____

Hyphens

Understand how hyphens can be used.

Background knowledge

Hyphens are generally used to join two words together to make a compound word, such as 'step-brother' and 'fat-free'. However, most compound words do not have hyphens in them, such as 'football' and 'sunrise'. It is important that children are introduced to the term hyphen understand how and when to use one to avoid ambiguity, for example with 'resent' (to feel bitter) and 're-sent' (to send again), or 'recover' (to return to normal) and 're-cover' (to cover again).

Activities

● **Photocopiable page 113 'Sports day'**
This activity plays with the idea of mock hyphenated words, asking children to construct a list of imaginary activities for a sports day using hyphenated words. They then have to show their understanding of the use of hyphens to connect words by inventing equipment that will be used in the sports. This equipment must have a hyphenated name.

● **Photocopiable page 114 'Make it make sense'**
We use the hyphen as a way to avoid ambiguity or confusion over the meaning of some words. For instance, the hyphen helps us distinguish whether we should 'resign' or 're-sign'. In this activity, the children have work out what the sentences mean when they do not contain hyphens and where the hyphens should go to remove the ambiguity.

● **Photocopiable page 115 'I resent that!'**
The prefix 're', can cause problems of ambiguity. There are a number of words that start with 're' but have different pronunciations when a hyphen is added after the 're'. The first task asks the children to differentiate between the meanings of similar words and to demonstrate their understanding by inserting them correctly in sentences. The correct answers are 're-mark' and 'recover'. The second task requires the children to insert the hyphens in the correct places and to explain the meanings of the words by using them in appropriate sentences.

Further ideas

● **Finding hyphens:** Ask the children to use a dictionary to find various words with hyphens. They can also compare different dictionaries – words will be hyphenated in some but not in others. Explain that over time hyphenated words can lose their hyphen (such as 'haystack').

● **Remember, remember:** Ask the children to work in pairs to think of as many words as they can with the prefix 're'. They may come up with words such as 'reply', 'revise', 'remember' and 'renew'. Ask the children to explain why these words do not have hyphens in them but other words, such as 're-sent', do.

● **Log in:** Ask the children to keep a log of when they discover hyphens in their reading. Ask them to record the type of book they were reading, such as fiction or non-fiction. Can they see any links between the types of book?

Digital content

On the digital component you will find:
● Printable versions of all three photocopiable pages.
● Answers to 'Make it make sense' and 'I resent that!'.

Hyphens

Sports day

■ Copy the words from the box, arranging them in different orders and putting in hyphens to create some new games for a sports day.

For example: balance-the-shark

eat	the	shark
throw	a	teacher
balance	my	elephant
hunt	your	bus
chase	an	egg

The games

■ Next invent equipment for the sports by connecting words with hyphens.

The equipment

Name:

Hyphens

Make it make sense

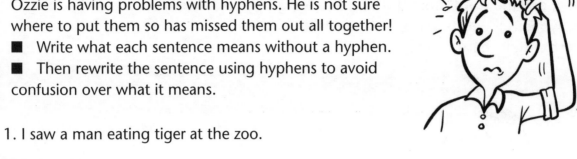

Ozzie is having problems with hyphens. He is not sure where to put them so has missed them out all together!

■ Write what each sentence means without a hyphen.

■ Then rewrite the sentence using hyphens to avoid confusion over what it means.

1. I saw a man eating tiger at the zoo.

This means: _____

Ozzie should have written:

_____

2. I've written thirty odd books.

This means: _____

Ozzie should have written:

_____

3. Father to be hit on head by falling tree.

This means: _____

Ozzie should have written:

_____

4. The prime minister gave a talk to small business owners.

This means: _____

Ozzie should have written:

_____

5. Everyone cheered when her dart went straight into the bull's eye.

This means: _____

Ozzie should have written:

_____

Hyphens

I resent that!

■ Choose the correct words to write in the gaps to make these sentences make sense.
■ Then write a sentence using the other word.

1. The examiner had to _____ all the essays.

   remark   re-mark

_____

_____

2. It took me a whole day to _____ from the cross-country run.

   recover   re-cover

_____

_____

■ Rewrite the words below with a hyphen to change their meanings.
■ Then write two sentences using each word once.

3. **Reform** _____

_____

_____

4. **Resort** _____

_____

_____

5. **Resent** _____

_____

_____

Using punctuation

Objective

Apply knowledge of punctuation.

Background knowledge

These activities revise some of the main points of punctuation that children should be developing an understanding of, notably:

● **capital letter:** at the start of a sentence; for proper nouns (names of people, places, the days of the week); for the personal pronoun 'I'
● **full stop:** to demarcate sentences
● **question mark:** to denote a question
● **inverted commas:** to demarcate speech
● **comma:** to separate clauses; to separate items in a list; to clarify meaning or avoid ambiguity in writing; after fronted adverbials
● **exclamation mark:** to show an exclamation
● **colon:** to introduce a list or to introduce a second independent clause
● **semicolon:** to provide a stronger pause than a comma, separating clauses
● **apostrophe:** to show possession or contraction
● **dash:** to mark the boundary between independent clauses; to use around a parenthetical clause
● **hyphen:** to join a prefix to a root word; to avoid ambiguity.

Activities

● **Photocopiable page 117 'Punctuation checklist'**
This checklist provides an opportunity for children to consolidate their knowledge of the punctuation marks they have covered. It asks them to identify when they have seen them being used in writing. Share a range of texts in the classroom, asking the children to find examples of the punctuation and reflect on their use, based on the context in which they encounter them. Then ask them to complete the table.

● **Photocopiable page 118 'What goes where?'**
This sheet assesses the children's ability to use the punctuation marks they have been taught. The children have to show their understanding by rewriting sentences using the correct punctuation marks.
● **Photocopiable page 119 'Finding punctuation'**
Ask the children to try to punctuate the first text before they look at the second one. In pairs, ask the children to discuss the problems caused by the lack of punctuation.

Further ideas

● **Apostrophes:** Ask the children to write definitions for apostrophes of contraction and apostrophes of possession. They need to give an example for each one. Then ask them to expand their writing by creating a paragraph containing at least two examples of each apostrophe. They should then swap their writing with a partner who will check the accuracy.
● **The contents:** Give the children a contents page from a non-fiction text. Ask the children to rewrite the page as a bullet point list. Remind them to include a colon at the start of the list. Encourage the children to write the list again, but this time in continuous prose using a colon, semicolons and commas. Lead on to a discussion about which list was the easier to write and to understand. More confident learners could be invited to write explanations for their thoughts.
● **Recipe book:** Give the children a list in prose of the ingredients for a simple recipe, such as for bread. Also, give them a bullet point list of the cooking instructions. Ask the children to rewrite the list so that the ingredients are in a bullet list and the instructions are written in a paragraph.

Digital content

On the digital component you will find:
● Printable versions of all three photocopiable pages.
● Answers to 'Punctuation checklist' and 'What goes where?'.
● Interactive version of 'What goes where?'.

Using punctuation

Punctuation checklist

■ In the table below, write the correct punctuation marks in the symbol column.

■ Write a short explanation for each punctuation mark in the function column.

■ When you have seen this used in text you have read put a tick in the final column. The first row has been completed for you as an example.

!	( )	;	,	'	?	.	-	–	A	" "	:

Punctuation mark	Symbol	Function	Seen it?
Question mark	?	Shows that the sentence is a question.	
Capital letter			
Full stop			
Inverted commas (speech marks)			
Brackets			
Comma			
Exclamation mark			
Colon			
Semicolon			
Dash			
Apostrophe			
Hyphen			

SCHOLASTIC
www.scholastic.co.uk　　PHOTOCOPIABLE　　Scholastic English Skills
Grammar and punctuation: Year 6　　117

Name:

Using punctuation

What goes where?

■ Rewrite each of these sentences using the punctuation shown in the box alongside them.

1. the room was painted in many colours
blue green bright pink and yellow

_____

_____

| capital letter |
| colon |
| two commas |
| full stop |

2. the fifth of may my birthday is only three days away

_____

_____

| two capital letters |
| brackets |
| full stop |

3. as the alligator which had escaped from the zoo
slipped into the classroom the children shouted help help

_____

_____

| three capital letters |
| four commas |
| inverted commas |
| (speech marks) |
| two exclamation |
| marks |

4. jacks worst nightmare came true when the teacher asked
can you sing a solo in assembly

_____

_____

| two capital letters |
| apostrophe |
| comma |
| inverted commas |
| (speech marks) |
| question mark |

5. i stopped reading something was outside and went to the
window

_____

_____

| capital letter |
| two dashes |
| full stop |

6. the teams were equally matched a draw was a fair result

_____

_____

| capital letter |
| semicolon |
| full stop |

Using punctuation

Finding punctuation

■ Try to punctuate the first passage below. Then check your changes against the second passage.

■ In pairs, discuss the problems caused by the lack of punctuation in the first passage.

davids omelettes

david makes brilliant omelettes davids recipe uses the following two eggs a little bit of butter grated cheese and one finely chopped mushroom it has to be chopped into really little bits and fried beforehand

    first take an egg beater and beat the eggs they dont need to be very well beaten then melt the butter in a small frying pan dont let the butter get too hot pour the beaten egg mixture into the pan when it is nearly solid turn it over and sprinkle the mushrooms over it then quickly add the grated cheese and fold the omelette into the shape of a semicircle let the cheese melt for a few moments take care the omelette doesnt overcook

    david says a good omelette is not a snack my recipe its a meal in itself what do you think

David's omelettes

David makes brilliant omelettes. David's recipe uses the following: two eggs, a little bit of butter, grated cheese and one finely chopped mushroom (it has to be chopped into really little bits and fried beforehand).

    First take an egg-beater and beat the eggs; they don't need to be very well beaten. Then melt the butter in a small frying pan (don't let the butter get too hot!). Pour the beaten egg mixture into the pan. When it is nearly solid, turn it over and sprinkle the mushrooms over it. Then quickly add the grated cheese and fold the omelette into the shape of a semicircle. Let the cheese melt for a few moments; take care the omelette doesn't overcook.

    David says, "A good omelette is not a snack. My recipe – it's a meal in itself." What do you think?

Punctuation in writing

Secure the use of a wide range of punctuation in writing.

Writing focus

Building on previous activities, this section encourages children to use a wide variety of punctuation for different purposes in their writing.

Skills to writing

● **Punctuation in context**

Having ascertained the use of the range of punctuation marks, children now need to apply them to a range of texts. Children should be encouraged to explain the usage. For example, if a colon is used, they need to see whether it starts a list or introduces speech. Ask the children to read the first two pages of *Carrie's War* by Nina Bawden – apart from being a great opening, it's also awash with a variety of punctuation. Ask the children to find examples of punctuation from their reading and to write explanations of how their use helps the reader to understand the text. In particular, ask them to look for examples of punctuation around parenthesis and to explain why dashes, brackets, ellipsis or commas have been used.

● **Conjunction or comma?**

Children need to be encouraged to review the sentences they write that use conjunctions for connecting clauses. Encourage them to consider if could they use a comma or semicolon instead.

● **What can we use instead?**

Some punctuation marks, particularly dashes, can be used in a variety of ways and can often replace others. For example, these three versions are equally acceptable: *Tomorrow, May 12th, is my birthday*; *Tomorrow – May 12th – is my birthday*; *Tomorrow (May 12th) is my birthday*. The dash can also be used instead of ellipsis points: *I heard a noise outside…I decided to look*; *I*

heard a noise outside – I decided to look. Give the children examples of these sentences and similar, and ask them to rewrite them with alternative punctuation.

● **Replacing the colon**

Remind the children of the main uses of colons. Ask them to choose one of them and to write a sentence using it. Then ask them to swap their sentence with a partner. The partner has to rewrite the sentence using a different, but equally valid, set of punctuation marks.

● **Pick a card – any card**

Make sets of flash cards with the following punctuation marks on them: colon, semicolon, hyphen and dash. You will need at least four examples of each punctuation mark for each set. Ask the children to work in groups of four. The children shuffle the cards and place them face down on the table. One child picks a card at random. Another child has ten seconds to give a definition of the term. The other two children have 30 seconds to write a sentence containing the punctuation mark. When this is completed, the children change roles and play the game again. You can expand this into a whole-class challenge by dividing the class into two equal-ability groups and reading the flash cards yourself. Each group takes it in turns to answer. If they are right they get one point. The winning team is the one that has the most points after five definitions.

Activities

● **Photocopiable page 122 'The Elves and the Shoemaker'**

This text contains a number of colons and semicolons – more than writers would use today. Ask the children to read the story in groups, looking closely at how the colons and semicolons are being used. Where might they not have been used if the text had been written today? Help the children to understand the functions that the colons and semicolons are performing. They should consider the way these marks prompt them to pause – how different are they from full stops? It is interesting to see how colons and semicolons have 'separated out' from each other in their usage in modern writing, having much more clearly defined functions. In 'The Elves and the Shoemaker' many of the colons would be substituted for a dash today (for example: *As for the shoemaker – he lived well the rest of his life*). Other colons might be replaced by full stops, especially in writing for young children (*We must do something for them. We shall make them some clothes and boots to keep them warm*) or semicolons (*Each night the shoemaker cut out his shoes; each morning he returned to find them expertly finished*).

Ask the children to choose three different sentences from the text that use colons. They should then rewrite the sentences using alternative punctuation marks. For each sentence, they should write an explanation of why they have used the new punctuation marks, whether they think their version is an improvement or not and give reasons for their thinking.

● **Photocopiable page 123 'Pauline's Perfect Punctuation'**

This activity will assess the children's ability to use colons, semicolons, hyphens and dashes accurately. The children have to add the details to complete the sections of Pauline's book by giving examples to fit each of the blank sections. For example, for something with two dashes in it to show a break in a train of thought, they might write: *I was wondering – I often did – how to answer the question*. The task does not require the children to define the terms or devices.

Write on

● **Hyphenated names**

Challenge the children to devise some interesting characters using hyphenated names, a bit like the odd games devised on photocopiable page 113 'Sports day'. What sort of character is Soup-Snaffler? A character like Child-Guzzler is obviously one to avoid, but what about Pirate-Teacher? Once they have devised their hyphenated names, invite the children to swap characters around and plan out adventures in which one of their characters meets a character devised by another child. Let them write out their stories as a paired writing activity.

● **Advertise it**

Divide the children into groups of four. Give each group a punctuation mark. Ask them to draft a 20-second television advertisement for their punctuation mark. They should explain why their audience should 'buy' their product. The children can perform their pieces for the rest of the class.

● **You look familiar**

In pairs, ask the children to write a script for an interview between a talk-show host and a punctuation mark. The opening line from the host is, *"You look familiar but I can't remember your name."* He/she then has to ask a series of questions about the shape of the punctuation mark and its usage. The punctuation mark gives appropriate replies but cannot mention its name. The pairs should perform their script for the rest of the children who have to guess which punctuation mark is being interviewed.

● **It takes two**

Ask the children to work in pairs. Each pair needs to produce a sentence that contains two of the following: colon, semicolon, dash, hyphen. They then swap their sentences with another pair to peer assess each others' work. This could also be done with more extended pieces of writing.

Digital content

On the digital component you will find:
● Printable versions of both photocopiable pages.

Name:

Punctuation in writing

The Elves and the Shoemaker

■ The use of punctuation changes over time. Sometimes older texts, like this one by the Brothers Grimm, contain more punctuation marks than modern texts. Read the story, find the colons and semicolons and look at how they are being used.

There was once an honest shoemaker who worked very hard; but no matter how much he worked, he never earned enough to live. At last he had nothing left in the world but a small piece of leather: just enough to make one final pair of shoes. The shoemaker cut the shoes out carefully and laid them out on his bench; they would be ready for when he returned in the morning. That night he said his prayers as usual and slept peacefully.

What a surprise greeted him next day: there on the workbench, was the most beautiful pair of shoes the shoemaker had ever seen! Every stitch was perfect; the craftsmanship was faultless. Later that day a gentleman came into the shop and asked to try the shoes. Imagine: they fitted him perfectly and he was so pleased that he paid handsomely for them. Now the shoemaker could buy more leather.

And so the days continued. Each night the shoemaker cut out his shoes: each morning he returned to find them expertly finished. He began to grow prosperous again.

One evening around Christmas time, the shoemaker made a decision: 'I want to stay up tonight,' he said to his wife, 'to see just who is making my shoes for me.' So they hid themselves in the workroom and waited.

At the stroke of midnight they heard the sound of tiny feet scuttling across the floor: two, tiny, naked men scrambled up to the shoemaker's bench, where they sat and began to sew and stitch the pieces of leather; working so swiftly that in no time at all they had finished the shoes. Then the two little men disappeared as quickly as they had come.

The shoemaker and his wife were astonished: they had never imagined that elves had been helping them. 'Those two little men have made us wealthy, husband,' said the wife. 'We must do something for them: we shall make them some clothes and boots to keep them warm.'

When the little men came that night, they fell on the clothing with delight; they quickly dressed themselves and danced and capered about the workroom – and right out of the door, never to be seen again.

As for the shoemaker: he lived well the rest of his life.

Retold by Jackie Andrews

■SCHOLASTIC
www.scholastic.co.uk

Punctuation in writing

Pauline's Perfect Punctuation

Pauline is an author who is trying to write a book called *Pauline's Perfect Punctuation*. However, she is struggling with one section. She needs to show how colons, semicolons, dashes and hyphens are used. She has some ideas for pages and has written them below.

■ Help her to complete the pages by writing examples in the spaces below.

1. A list of punctuation marks using bullet points:

_____

_____

_____

_____

_____

2. A list of three hyphenated words with their meanings. This list should use semicolons to separate the words:

_____

_____

_____

_____

3. Two equal clauses separated by a semicolon:

_____

_____

4. A sentence with two dashes in it to show a break in a train of thought:

_____

_____

Chapter 6

Getting to grips with grammar

Introduction

This chapter is a general revision and consolidation of the work that has been done on word forms. The children will revisit word classes, identify different forms of clauses and sentences and experiment with their usage to enhance their writing. For further practice, please see the 'Getting to grips with grammar' section of the Year 6 workbook.

In this chapter

Revision of word classes page 127	Revisit different words classes and consider their functions in sentences.
More on word classes page 131	Revisit different words classes and consider their functions in sentences.
Sentences page 135	Identify sentences with different forms and learn to use them in writing.
Combining words, phrases and clauses page 139	Use different kinds of clause in writing and combine words, phrases and clauses using a variety of conjunctions.
Words at work page 143	Experiment with word classes, clauses and conjunctions to improve sentence writing.

Poster notes

Word classes (page 125)
Word classes are sometimes called 'parts of speech' – the children need to be familiar with both terms. The poster presents each word class with examples. Ask children to give a definition of each class to ensure that they understand the differences. Can they complete the poster's statement about frogs? Discuss with the children why it was not possible to complete the original sentence without using some word classes twice. Challenge the children to write the longest sentence they can without using any word classes twice. They will soon discover that it is difficult to write extended sentences without using nouns twice.

Sentence forms (page 126)
This poster presents the four forms of sentence. It gives definitions for each type of sentence and an example. Lead a discussion on how the punctuation helps the children to recognise the type of sentence. Then focus on the use of the exclamation marks in the command and the exclamation sentences. Ask the children to consider how the vocabulary in these two sentences makes it obvious which is a command and which is an exclamation.

Vocabulary

Children should already know:
adjective, adverb, command, conjunction, determiner, exclamation, noun, preposition, pronoun, question, statement, verb

Getting to grips with grammar

Sentence forms

STATEMENT

This car is so slow.

Definition: Gives information.

QUESTION

Why is this car so slow?

Definition: Asks for information.

COMMAND

Slow down!

Definition: Gives an order or a command.

EXCLAMATION

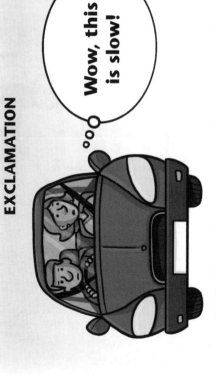

Wow, this is slow!

Definition: Expresses surprise, anger or emotion.

Revision of word classes

Objective

Revisit different words classes and consider their functions in sentences.

Background knowledge

The children need to be familiar with all of the word classes and sentence forms: noun (naming word: common noun – *table*; proper noun – *Thursday*; countable – *boy*; non-countable – *money*); verb (doing word; states actions, feelings or events); adjective (describes a noun); adverb (modifies a verb, an adjective, another adverb or even a whole clause); preposition (links a noun, pronoun or noun phrase to another part of a sentence); determiner (specifies a noun as known or unknown – *the*, *a*, *some*, *every*); pronoun (normally used like a noun but is harder to modify – *she talked to him*); conjunction (links two words or clauses together); statement (a sentence type that gives information); question (a sentence type that asks for information); exclamation (a sentence type that expresses surprise, anger or emotion); command (a sentence type that gives an order or command).

Activities

● **Photocopiable page 128 'Word insert'**
Adjectives modify nouns but adverbs are trickier to spot. Adverbs do not just modify verbs. They can modify a verb, an adjective, another adverb or even a whole clause. The sentences in this activity work without being modified but it can demonstrate the way in which modifiers can add to a piece of writing.
● **Photocopiable page 129 'Make it more detailed'**
This activity asks the children to experiment with using word classes within a piece of writing. They are asked to insert more exciting verbs, adverbs and adjectives to make the writing more interesting. It could be done once without a thesaurus and then redrafted using one. At the end, the children have to explain why they chose some of the vocabulary.

● **Photocopiable page 130 'Sentence sorter'**
In pairs, the children start by matching words to their word classes. They then use these words in the sentence sorter to generate various nonsensical sentences. Finally, the children should discuss how their choice of adverbs, prepositions and adjectives affects the reader's thoughts about the verbs and nouns.

Further ideas

● **Talkers:** Can the children think of anyone on TV whose speech is particularly noticeable? It could be someone who complains all the time or talks too quickly. Encourage them to listen to the speech of this person and see which word classes dominate their speech.
● **Adverb of the week:** On a display board, write a simple verb, such as 'walked'. Ask the children to add appropriate adverbs during the week. At the end of the week, discuss the adverb choices with the children, highlighting how each would alter our understanding of the verb. Have a new word the next week. To stretch their vocabulary, do not allow them to use any of the adverbs from the previous week.
● **What's it like and where is it?:** This activity has its focus on adverbs, adjectives and prepositions. Make a set of flash cards of everyday nouns, such as 'house', 'car', 'clock'. Working in pairs, one child turns over a card and the other child has to make up a sentence including the noun, an adverb, an adjective and a preposition. For example, if the card had clock written on it, the second child might say: *The accurate clock is on the dirty wall*. The children take it in turns to make up the sentences. They are not allowed to use any of the adverbs, adjectives or prepositions used previously.

Digital content

On the digital component you will find:
● Printable versions of all three photocopiable pages.
● Answers to 'Sentence sorter'.
● Interactive version of 'Sentence sorter'.

Name:

Revision of word classes

Word insert

■ Cut out these sentences.

■ Split them in places where you could add an adjective or adverb.

| I walked to the house. | | I | walked to the | house. |

■ Cut out small strips of paper. Make some inserts. Use these to add adjectives and adverbs. Try to use unusual ones.

| I | **carefully** | walked to the | **creepy** | house. |

Our team played in a football match.

The burglar threw his torch at the alarm.

My brother kicked the football.

I walked past the house.

We slipped into the door.

The mouse ran from the cat.

The man left his house.

The work was finished so the girl gave it to the teacher.

The dog ran up the path towards the man.

The children walked down the corridor into the assembly.

Revision of word classes

Make it more detailed

■ Look at the section from the story below. In pairs, for each of the verbs in bold, think of three more exciting ones. Choose one and write it above the original verb.

■ In the spaces with the dotted lines (.............................), insert an interesting adverb.

■ In the spaces with the complete lines (_____), insert a really imaginative adjective. You cannot use any of your new words twice.

"Robin," she **said** .... "Behind you!"

The outlaw **turned** round .... as three

of the Sheriff's _____ guards **came** down the

_____ steps towards him. They **had** their

_____ swords over their heads and **went**

.... towards the outlaw.

Marion .... took hold of Robin's hand and **went**

through the castle window, **going** into the _____

moat below. As they **went** down into the murky depths he **hoped** for

air but the _____ weeds of the moat **went** around

his legs. Suddenly a hand **held** the scruff of his neck and **got** him

.... from the water. Marion put him onto her horse

and **went** up behind him. They went off into the forest. Behind them, the

Sheriff **said** .... to his guards, "**Go** after them and

bring them back, dead or alive!"

Name:

Revision of word classes

Sentence sorter

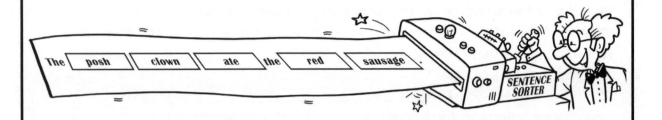

■ In pairs, cut out the words below. Sort them into their word classes using the sorting table at the bottom of the page.

■ See what strange sentences you can make up by putting the words into the sentence sorter above.

■ Discuss how the use of the adverbs, prepositions and adjectives changes our thoughts about the nouns and verbs.

red	tasty	behind	regularly	cupboard
threw	chased	voraciously	above	hid
across	over	huge	ate	willingly
sausage	happily	watched	posh	under
viciously	clown	princess	wall	brilliant

Verbs	Adverbs	Adjectives	Prepositions	Nouns

More on word classes

Objective

Revisit different words classes and consider their functions in sentences.

Background knowledge

This section is a continuation of the previous one. The children will need to know about the word classes and sentence forms: noun, verb, adjective, adverb, preposition, determiner, pronoun, conjunction, question, exclamation and command. Ensure that the children are clear about the uses of them all. This will give them valuable further experience of working with the different word classes and sentence forms to enhance their written pieces by encouraging them to extend the variety of their writing.

Activities

● **Photocopiable page 132 'Missing words'**
This is an oral activity for children working together in pairs to try to read the content of two passages with access to different types of words. You will need to cut the sheet into texts (a) and (b) for each passage. Firstly, the children look at text (a), which will probably help very little. Next, they hand text (a) back in and receive text (b). This is much easier to reconstruct. Having completed this they can look at the two texts together and try to read the passage. They should then discuss which word classes were missing from each extract and which were the most difficult to insert.

● **Photocopiable page 133 'Word classes in use'**
The key to making this activity work is to select good portions of TV to watch. Obscure and clearly defined pieces, such as the pre-race discussion of horses can provide the sort of snippet. They don't need to be long. The children need to record the word classes and then try to analyse them to identify patterns.

● **Photocopiable page 134 'Bleak House'**
The children are given a passage from Charles Dickens' *Bleak House*. The setting presented is a powerful description of a London scene. The children are asked to comment on specific word classes in the text. Once they have done this, they can choose their own examples to analyse.

Further ideas

● **How near is it?:** Give the children the name of an object that they will all recognise, such as: *the school hall*. Ask them to work in pairs to come up with as many ways as possible of explaining where it is using prepositions.

● **Spaghetti conjunction:** Ask the children to research, using the internet, to find as many conjunctions as they can. On a large piece of paper, ask the children to make a 'spaghetti conjunction' by writing them on the page, starting in the centre and working outwards. Then ask them to try to devise a simple sentence including a conjunction and to use two of the alternatives on the sheet to replace it.

● **Conjunction tennis:** Having made the 'spaghetti conjunction' in the previous activity, ask the children to play 'conjunction tennis'. In pairs, the children take it in turns to 'serve' a conjunction, which has to be 'returned' by another conjunction. Play continues until one player cannot 'return'. The person who gave the last conjunction gets one point and serves the next conjunction. Conjunctions cannot be repeated during any one 'rally'. The first player to five points is the winner.

Digital content

On the digital component you will find:
● Printable versions of all three photocopiable pages.

Name:

More on word classes

Missing words

■ Cut out the texts and read the passages separately. There are words missing – can you make sense of the passages?

✂ -

(Invention a)

The _____ _____ was _____ in _____. _____ of _____ was _____ around _____ . He _____ the _____ _____ _____. In his _____ _____ _____ _____ of _____ _____ out of a _____. These _____ _____ a _____. It was _____ as a _____.

(Invention b)

_____ steam engine _____ invented _____ Africa. Hero _____ Alexandria _____ born _____ 20CE. _____ invented _____ first steam engine. _____ _____ simple machine two jets _____ steam spurted _____ _____ _____ container. _____ jets turned _____ sphere. _____ _____ used _____ _____ toy.

(Body a)

_____ are _____ by _____ _____ the _____ of our _____. When the _____ _____ it can _____ the _____ _____ under the _____. They _____ _____ and this _____ up as a _____ _____. This is a _____. The _____ is _____ up of _____ _____ from _____ _____ and _____. If the _____ is _____ the _____ can _____ up to _____ a _____.

(Body b)

Bruises _____ made _____ objects hitting _____ flesh _____ _____ bodies. _____ _____ object hits _____ _____ damage _____ blood vessels _____ _____ skin. _____ release blood _____ _____ shows _____ _____ _____ purple patch. _____ _____ _____ bruise. _____ bruise _____ made _____ _____ fluid released _____ blood vessels _____ cells. _____ _____ head _____ struck _____ bruise _____ swell _____ _____ make _____ bump.

PHOTOCOPIABLE

■SCHOLASTIC
www.scholastic.co.uk

More on word classes

Word classes in use

■ Watch some different types of television such as:

A weather forecast   A sports report   An advert   A presenter talking to younger children

■ Watch the same type of broadcast more than once. Make a note of the word classes that are being used and add them to the table below.

■ Note them on the chart below.

Well, Brian, I gently tapped the ball past their defence and dribbled it into an open goal.

Look out for words that are special to that type of programme!

	Pronouns	Nouns	Conjunctions	Prepositions	Adverbs
Weather forecast					
Sports report					
Advert					
Presenter (young children)					

■ What similarities or differences can you see in the word classes used in each programme?

More on word classes

Bleak House

- Read this opening section from *Bleak House* by Charles Dickens.

CHAPTER 1

London. Michaelmas term lately over, and the Lord Chancellor sitting in Lincoln's Inn Hall. Implacable November weather. As much mud in the streets, as if the waters had but newly retired from the face of the earth, and it would not be wonderful to meet a Megalosaurus, forty feet long or so, waddling like an elephantine lizard up Holborn Hill. Smoke lowering down from chimney-pots, making a soft black drizzle with flakes of soot in it as big as full-grown snowflakes – gone into mourning, one might imagine, for the death of the sun. Dogs, undistinguishable in mire. Horses, scarcely better; splashed to their very blinkers. Foot passengers, jostling one another's umbrellas, in a general infection of ill temper, and losing their foot-hold at street-corners, where tens of thousands of other foot passengers have been slipping and sliding since the day broke (if this day ever broke), adding new deposits to the crust upon crust of mud, sticking at those points tenaciously to the pavement, and accumulating at compound interest.

- Think about the language use. In the table below, write down what you think makes these words special, interesting or unusual.

Verbs: jostling	
Adjectives: elephantine	
Adverbs: tenaciously	
Preposition: crust upon crust	

Sentences

Identify sentences with different forms and learn to use them in writing.

Background knowledge

There are four main sentence forms:
● **Statement:** a sentence that gives information – *This is right.*
● **Question:** a sentence that asks for information – *Is this right?*
● **Exclamation:** a sentence that expresses surprise, anger or emotion – *It's right!*
● **Command:** a sentence that gives an order or command – *Get it right!*

Activities

● **Photocopiable page 136 'Sentence forms'**
This task asks the children to sort examples of sentences into statements, questions, exclamations and commands. This will enable you to assess their understanding of the different forms.
● **Photocopiable page 137 'Making different forms of sentences'**
This activity asks the children to use many of the word classes with which they have become familiar. Using words from the table, the children make a sentence in one form and then change it into the other three forms. It does not matter which form of sentence they choose for their first one.
● **Photocopiable page 138 'The trouble with sentences'**
The children are given a transcript of a teacher introducing the topic of sentences. They have to deconstruct the passage into the different sentence forms. They then have to consider how changing the punctuation could alter some of the sentence forms.

Further ideas

● **Sentence spotting:** Ask children to look for different sentence forms around them and see which are most common in certain contexts, such as comics, street signs, notices and so on. Make a large display and ask the children to write their sentences under the four headings: statement, question, exclamation and command. Discuss whether one form is predominant. Ask the children why they think this might be.
● **Which sentence am I?:** Divide the children into groups of four. Each child will represent a different sentence form. Ask them to script a conversation between them all. Each child can only speak in their form of sentence. Ask the children to present their conversations to the rest of the class. The other children must then try to identify which person is using which sentence form. For example:
  ● *"Today we are going to talk about sentences."*
  ● *"Why?"*
  ● *"It's rude to interrupt!"*
  ● *"Get on with it!"*
● **What's the order?:** Working in pairs, ask the children to write a piece of dialogue containing only four sentences, one of each form. They then cut the sentences up and pass them to another pair. The new pair has to reorganise the sentences in the correct order and explain, using the correct terminology, which sentence form is which and why they have chosen their order.

Digital content

On the digital component you will find:
● Printable versions of all three photocopiable pages.
● Answers for all three photocopiable pages.
● Interactive version of 'Sentence forms'.

Name:

Sentences

Sentence forms

There are four forms of sentence:

Statement	Question	Exclamation	Command
Gives information.	Asks for information.	Expresses surprise, anger or emotion.	Gives an order or command.
This car is so slow.	Why is this car so slow?	Wow, that's slow!	Slow down!

■ Sort out these sentences into the correct forms at the bottom of the page and rewrite them in the table and add the missing punctuation.

Who said that	Why can't we	I like strawberries	That's fantastic
Brilliant	It's Tuesday	Oh no	What is for dinner
My brother has come home	Don't touch it	How tall is Blackpool Tower	Do not talk in the exams
Be careful	I can't believe you said that	Stand still	Yesterday was wet

Statements	Questions
Exclamations	**Commands**

Sentences

Making different forms of sentences

■ Identify the correct sentence form for each of the sentences below.

1. I can write it correctly.

_____

2. Can you write it correctly?

_____

3. You've written it correctly!

_____

4. Write it correctly!

_____

■ Choose at least one verb, two nouns, a pronoun, an adjective, a preposition and a determiner from the box below to create a sentence in any of the forms.

Verbs	Nouns	Pronouns	Adjectives	Prepositions	Determiners
make	shoes	I	hairy	in	the
find	dog	my	beautiful	over	one
go	car	our	strange	behind	a

■ Then rewrite it in each of the other three forms. You can change the form of the verb if it helps you. For example, you could use 'made' instead of 'make'.

Statement:

_____

Question:

_____

Exclamation:

_____

Command:

_____

Name:

Sentences

The trouble with sentences

■ Read the passage below. It's a teacher talking to the class about sentences, but not everything is going to plan!

"Today we are going to talk about sentence construction. I know I said construction, George, but stop throwing those building blocks at Henry. Now, there are four different forms of sentence: statement, question, exclamation and command. George, stop kicking Rebecca's chair. Why? Well, she doesn't like it. How do I know? She's crying. Oh that's very kind, Charlotte! She'll feel a lot better now. I'm surprised at you, George. Now, can we get back to sentences? Thank goodness for that! Listen carefully and look at me."

■ All four forms of sentences are in the passage. Identify them and write them in the correct boxes below.

Statements	Questions
Exclamations	**Commands**

Combining words, phrases and clauses

Objective

Use different kinds of clause in writing and combine words, phrases and clauses using a variety of conjunctions.

Background knowledge

This section concentrates on using clauses and conjunctions. There are a number of different clauses: independent clause, subordinate clause, relative clause. There are two forms of conjunctions: subordinating and coordinating.

- **Independent clauses:** An independent, or main, clause always contains at least a verb and a subject.
- **Subordinate clauses:** A clause that is dependent on another part of the same sentence. There are different forms of subordinate clause including relative and adverbial.
- **Relative clauses:** Relative clauses are a form of subordinate clause. They begin with 'who', 'which', 'where', 'when', 'whose', 'that' or with an implied (omitted) relative pronoun.
- **Subordinating conjunctions:** These introduce a subordinate clause.
- **Coordinating conjunctions:** These link two words or phrases together as a single pair.
  In addition, children need to know how modifying nouns and preposition phrases work.
- **Modifying nouns:** Nouns that modify other nouns by giving additional information about them.
- **Preposition phrases:** These are made up of a preposition and a noun phrase.

Activities

- **Photocopiable page 140 'Using conjunctions'**
This activity asks children to use a range of conjunctions in the middle of sentences to join words, phrases and clauses, using subordinating and coordinating conjunctions. The challenge is to construct a lengthy sentence using more than one conjunction.

- **Photocopiable page 141 'Conjunction sandwich'**
The children are given three different conjunctions – two subordinating and one coordinating. They have to write a sentence starter that will fit with all three, write appropriate endings and explore the effect that the different types of conjunctions have on the end of the sentences.
- **Photocopiable page 142 'Expand it'**
This activity will show the children how to build up complicated information concisely. They are given a picture of a spider. Around it are a number of adjectives. The children make an expanded noun phrase using them. The sentence is developed by the addition of a modifying noun before being completed by the addition of a preposition phrase.

Further ideas

- **Conjunction day:** Children can talk through the events of a day using as many conjunctions as they can think of. For example: *I went to the cloakroom because I forgot my dinner money.*
- **The longest:** Using the various conjunctions shown in these activities, children can try producing the longest sentence with the greatest number of conjunctions. For example: *Without thinking about what we were writing we produced this long sentence because our teacher set us the challenge but made out we wouldn't be able to do it yet we couldn't resist however…*
- **Thesaurus:** During their reading, ask the children to look for different conjunctions. Make a display of the children's words and ask them to use a thesaurus to find conjunctions with similar meanings that they could use to replace them.

Digital content

On the digital component you will find:
- Printable versions of all three photocopiable pages.

Name:

Combining words, phrases and clauses

Using conjunctions

■ Write sentences using conjunctions as in the examples shown below.

but	I wanted to play outside **but** it was time for tea.
and/but	I wanted to go outside **and** I asked my mum **but** she said it was time for tea.
because	
unless	
although/for	
since/after	
yet/or	
so/whenever	
as/though	
whereas/ when/until	

Conjunction sandwich

You are going to sandwich conjunctions between two clauses.

■   In the sentence starter box, write the beginning of a sentence that could be followed by a coordinating conjunction and then complete the sentence.

Sentence starter	
Coordinating conjunction	but
Continuation of sentence	

■   Use the same sentence starter. This time the link is a subordinating conjunction. Add a new ending to the sentence.

Sentence starter	
Subordinating conjunction	whenever
Continuation of sentence	

■   Repeat the process again, but this time the link is a subordinating conjunction that will create a relative clause after it.

Sentence starter	
Subordinating conjunction	that
Continuation of sentence	

■   How does the conjunction change the ending of each sentence?

_____

_____

Name:

Combining words, phrases and clauses

Expand it

You are going to build up a really detailed description.

■ Use at least two of the adjectives to build up an expanded noun phrase about a spider and write it below.

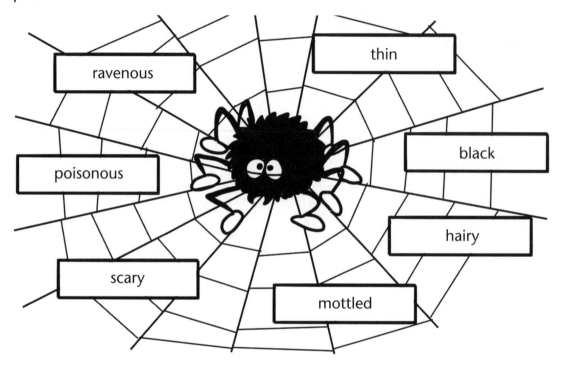

I saw a _____ spider.

■ Now add one of these modifying nouns to give more information about the spider. Where will your modifying noun fit into your sentence?

spotted-wolf funnel web	black widow	garden	tarantula	housepirate

I saw a _____ spider.

■ Finally, add some more detail using one of these preposition phrases at the end of the sentence.

in the kitchen	by the fridge	with an evil grin on its face	on my chair

I saw a _____ spider

.

■SCHOLASTIC
www.scholastic.co.uk

Words at work

Objective

Experiment with word classes, clauses and conjunctions to improve sentence writing.

Writing focus

Building on previous activities, this section encourages children to play around with different word classes, and to work creatively with clauses and conjunctions.

Skills to writing

● **Nouns, pronouns and conjunctions**

Ask the children to write a short piece in which they do not use any pronouns or conjunctions. They may well produce a series of short sentences that do not flow very well. Ask them to rewrite the piece, but this time they can only use each noun once. They have to use pronouns instead of the nouns on every subsequent occasion and they can link the sentences with conjunctions. Ask them to share both pieces of writing with a partner and to discuss the effect of the changes.

● **Find a clause**

Give the children an extract from a piece of writing. Ask them to identify sentences containing more than one clause. They should highlight the clauses in different colours and then decide if they are independent or subordinate clauses. They should then try to rewrite the clauses as two separate sentences containing independent clauses. This will enable them to identify the conjunction in the original sentence.

Activities

● **Photocopiable page 145 'Definite definitions'**

This activity will allow you to assess the children's understanding of the work done on parts of speech. The children are asked to write their own definitions and examples of a wide range of terms. The activity becomes progressively more complex.

● **Photocopiable page 146 'Right place, right pronoun'**

This activity is like a jigsaw. The children have to try reworking the sentences, splitting them and reshuffling to create new sentences. To get an answer that works out, they will need to work on a whole set of sentences, shuffling them around until they make sense. If they complete this activity successfully, they could work in pairs to create their own sentences and challenge other pairs to put them in the right order. Ask who can make the longest sentence using pronouns.

Write on

● **Dear Sir/Madam**
Create a letter, one word at a time. Start the activity (and the letter) with an opening such as 'Dear Head teacher'. Then invite one child at a time to contribute one word each to build the letter. For example: *I – am – writing – because – my…* This can result in a lot of adjectives being added (*I – am – writing – because – my – little – sad – scary…*), before someone offers up the noun (*I – am – writing – because – my – little – sad – scary – hamster…*). Continue adding words until you have an unusual letter. The letter should not be a long one. Once it is completed, ask the children to analyse the parts of it by using their definitions from photocopiable page 145 'Definite definitions' to categorise the word classes.

● **Protest**
Ask the children to think of something they would like to change. For example, would they like a longer playtime? Encourage them to come up with a cause for which they could mount a campaign. The first stage is a campaign poster. Ask them to use their knowledge of cohesive and presentational devices to create a list of all of the reasons their demands should be met. They then need to create a poster using conjunctions to link the ideas and to push home their argument.

● **Drafting support**
In pairs, ask the children to draft a letter to the person who they think could help their protest the most. This could be the head teacher, the prime minister or another important person. The letter should use all of the word classes the children have covered as well as appropriate punctuation. They should then share the letter with another pair. The second pair reads the letter and writes a reply as if they were the real recipient. They too should include all of the word classes and punctuation that they have covered. You may wish to help them by providing a checklist.

● **Why oh why?**
In pairs, give the children a word class. Ask them to write why we need that word class, a sentence containing it and what would happen if we didn't have that class. For example: *We use conjunctions to link nouns or clauses together. Example: Tomos went to the cinema but Angelika went ice-skating. If we did not use a conjunction we would have to use two sentences.* Display the work on the classroom wall and ask the children to use it as reference material when they are writing.

Digital content

On the digital component you will find:
● Printable versions of both photocopiable pages.
● Answers to 'Definite definitions' and 'Right place, right pronoun'.

Words at work

Definite definitions

■ Write your own brief definitions of some of the different word classes and give some examples for each one.

Pronoun	Preposition
Definition:	Definition:
Examples:	Examples:

Subordinating conjunction	Coordinating conjunction
Definition:	Definition:
Examples:	Examples:

■ Now write definitions of noun phrases and independent clauses and give one example for each.

Noun phrase	Independent clause
Definition:	Definition:
Example:	Example:

SCHOLASTIC
www.scholastic.co.uk   PHOTOCOPIABLE   Scholastic English Skills
Grammar and punctuation: Year 6   145

Name:

Words at work

Right place, right pronoun

■ The pronouns in these sentences are all mixed up. Cut them out and rearrange them so that the sentences make sense.

✂

| I think | herself | is the gate to | his | field. |

| I wonder | someone | is the name of | she | street? |

| Listen, | himself | is coming. |

| Mum said | this | wanted to be all by | what. |

| My little brother can tie | that | shoelaces by | this. |

Subject knowledge

1. Preliminary notes about grammar

Grammar involves the way in which words of different types are combined into sentences. The explanatory sections that follow will include definitions of types of word along with notes on how they are combined into sentences.

Three preliminary points about grammar:

- Function is all-important. Where a word is placed in relation to another word is crucial in deciding whether it is functioning as a verb or a noun. For example, the word 'run' will often be thought of as a verb. However, in a sentence like *They went for a run*, the word functions as a noun and the verb is 'went'.
- There are some consistencies in the way spelling is linked to grammar. For example, words like 'play' and 'shout' have the 'ed' ending to make past tense verbs, 'played' and 'shouted'. Adjectives like 'quick' and 'slow' take a 'ly' ending to make adverbs like 'quickly' and 'slowly'. There are exceptions to these rules but such consistencies can still prove useful when it comes to understanding the grammar of sentences.
- Nothing is sacred in language. Rules change over time; the double negative has gained currency, and regional variation in accent and dialect is now far more valued than has been the case in the past. The rules of grammar that follow are subject to change as the language we use lives and grows.

2. Words and functions

Grammar picks out the functions of words. The major classes or types of word in the English language are:

Noun
The name of something or someone, including concrete things, such as 'dog' or 'tree', and abstract things, such as 'happiness' or 'fear'.

Pronoun
A word that replaces a noun. The noun 'John' in *John is ill* can be replaced by a pronoun 'he', making *He is ill*.

Verb
A word that denotes an action or a happening. In the sentence *I ate the cake* the verb is 'ate'. These are sometimes referred to as 'doing' words.

Adjective
A word that modifies a noun. In the phrase *the little boat* the adjective 'little' describes the noun 'boat'.

Adverb

A word that modifies a verb. In the phrase *he slowly walked* the adverb is 'slowly'.

Preposition

A word or phrase that shows the relationship of one thing to another. In the phrase *the house beside the sea* the preposition 'beside' places the two nouns in relation to each other.

Conjunction

A word or phrase that joins other words and phrases. A simple example is the word 'and' that joins nouns in *Snow White and Doc and Sneezy*.

Determiner

Determiners appear before nouns and denote whether the noun is specific (*give me the book*) or not (*give me a book*). Note that 'the' (definite article) and 'a' or 'an' (indefinite articles) are the most common types of determiner.

Interjection

A word or phrase expressing or exclaiming an emotion, such as 'Oh!' and 'Aaargh!'
The various word types can be found in the following example sentences:

Lou	saw	his	new	house	from	the	train.
noun	verb	pronoun	adjective	noun	preposition	article	noun
Yeow!	I	hit	my	head	on	the	door.
interjection	pronoun	verb	pronoun	noun	preposition	article	noun
Amir	sadly	lost	his	bus fare	down	the	drain.
noun	adverb	verb	pronoun	noun	preposition	article	noun
Give	Jan	a	good	book	for	her	birthday.
verb	noun	article	adjective	noun	conjunction	pronoun	noun

The pages that follow provide more information on these word classes.

Nouns

There are four types of noun in English.

> A **noun** is the name of someone or something.

Common nouns are general names for things. For example, in the sentence *I fed the dog*, the noun 'dog' could be used to refer to any dog, not to a specific one. Other examples include 'boy', 'country', 'book', 'apple'.

Proper nouns are the specific names given to identify things or people. In a phrase like *Sam is my dog* the word 'dog' is the common noun but 'Sam' is a proper noun because it refers to and identifies a specific dog. Other examples include 'Wales' and 'Amazing Grace'.

Collective nouns refer to a group of things together, such as 'a flock (of sheep)' or 'a bunch (of bananas)'.

Abstract nouns refer to things that are not concrete, such as an action, a concept, an event, quality or state. Abstract nouns like 'happiness' and 'fulfilment' refer to ideas or feelings which are non-countable; others, such as 'hour', 'joke' and 'quantity' are countable.

Nouns can be singular or plural. To change a singular to a plural the usual rule is to add 's'. This table includes other rules to bear in mind:

If the singular ends in:	Rule	Examples
'y' after a consonant	Remove 'y', add 'ies'	party → parties
'y' after a vowel	add 's'	donkey → donkeys
'o' after a consonant	add 'es'	potato → potatoes
'o' after a vowel	add 's'	video → videos
an 's' sound such as 's', 'sh', 'x', 'z'	add 'es'	kiss → kisses dish → dishes
a 'ch' sound such as 'ch' or 'tch'	add 'es'	watch → watches church → churches

Pronouns

There are different classes of pronoun. These are the main types:

> A **pronoun** is a word that stands in for a noun.

Personal pronouns refer to people or things, such as 'I', 'you', 'it'. The personal pronouns distinguish between subject and object case ('I/me', 'he/him', 'she/her', 'we/us', 'they/them' and the archaic 'thou/thee').

Reflexive pronouns refer to people or things that are also the subject of the sentence. In the sentence *You can do this yourself* the pronoun 'yourself' refers to 'you'. Such pronouns end with 'self' or 'selves'. Other examples include 'myself', 'themselves'.

Possessive pronouns identify people or things as belonging to a person or thing. For example, in the sentence *The book is hers* the possessive pronoun 'hers' refers to 'the book'. Other examples include 'its' and 'yours'. Note that possessive pronouns never take an apostrophe.

Relative pronouns link relative clauses to their nouns. In the sentence *The man who was in disguise sneaked into the room* the relative clause 'who was in disguise' provides extra information about 'the man'. This relative clause is linked by the relative pronoun 'who'. Other examples include 'whom', 'which' and 'that'.

Interrogative pronouns are used in questions. They refer to the thing that is being asked about. In the question *What is your name?* and *Where is the book?* the pronouns 'what' and 'where' stand for the answers – the name and the location of the book.

Demonstrative pronouns are pronouns that 'point'. They are used to show the relation of the speaker to an object. There are four demonstrative pronouns in English 'this', 'that', 'these', 'those' used as in *This is my house* and *That is your house*. They have specific uses, depending upon the position of the object to the speaker:

	Near to speaker	Far away from speaker
Singular	this	that
Plural	these	those

Indefinite pronouns stand in for an indefinite noun. The indefinite element can be the number of elements or the nature of them but they are summed up in ambiguous pronouns such as 'any', 'some' or 'several'. Other examples are the pronouns that end with 'body', 'one' and 'thing', such as 'somebody', 'everyone' and 'anything'.

Person
Personal, reflexive and possessive pronouns can be in the first, second or third person.
- First-person pronouns ('I', 'we') involve the speaker or writer.
- Second-person pronouns ('you') refer to the listener or reader.
- Third-person pronouns refer to something other than these two participants in the communication ('he', 'she', 'it', 'they').

The person of the pronoun will agree with particular forms of verbs: 'I like'/'she likes'.

Verbs
The **tense** of a verb places a happening in time. The main tenses are the present and past.

A **verb** is a word that denotes an action or a happening.

English does not have a discrete future tense. It is made in a compound form using a present tense ('I will', 'I shall' and so on) and an infinitive (for example *I will go to the shops*).

The regular past tense is formed by the addition of the suffix 'ed', although some of the most common verbs in English have irregular past tenses.

Present tense (happening now)	Past tense (happened in past)	Future (to happen in future)
am, say, find, kick	was, said, found, kicked	will be, will say, shall find, shall kick

Continuous verbs
The present participle form of a verb is used to show a continuous action. Whereas a past tense like 'kicked' denotes an action that happened ('I kicked'), the present participle denotes the action as happening and continuing as it is described (*I was kicking*, the imperfect tense, or *I am kicking*, the present continuous). There is a sense in these uses of an action that has not ended.

The present participle usually ends in 'ing', such as 'walking', 'finding', and continuous verbs are made with a form of the verb 'be', such as 'was' or 'am': *I was running* and *I am running*.

Auxiliary verbs

Auxiliary verbs 'help' other verbs – they regularly accompany full verbs, always preceding them in a verb phrase. The auxiliary verbs in English can be divided into three categories:

Primary verbs are used to indicate the timing of a verb, such as 'be', 'have' or 'did' (including all their variations such as 'was', 'were', 'has', 'had' and so on). These can be seen at work in verb forms like *I was watching a film*, *He has finished eating*, *I didn't lose my keys*.

Modal verbs indicate the possibility of an action occurring or the necessity of it happening, such as *I might watch a film*, *I should finish eating* and *I shouldn't lose my keys*.

The modal verbs in English are: 'would', 'could', 'might', 'should', 'can', 'will', 'shall', 'may', and 'must'. These verbs never function on their own as main verbs. They always act as auxiliaries helping other verbs.

Marginal modals, namely 'dare', 'need', 'ought to' and 'used to'. These act as modals, such as in the sentences *I dared enter the room*, *You need to go away* and *I ought to eat my dinner*, but they can also act as main verbs, as in *I need cake*.

Adjectives

The main function of adjectives is to define quality or quantity. Examples of the use of descriptions of quality include 'good story', 'sad day' and 'stupid dog'. Examples of the use of descriptions of quantity include 'some stories', 'ten days' and 'many dogs'.

> An **adjective** is a word that modifies a noun.

Adjectives can appear in one of three different degrees of intensity. In the table below it can be seen that there are 'er' and 'est' endings that show an adjective is comparative or superlative, though, there are exceptions. The regular comparative is formed by the addition of the suffix 'er' to shorter words and 'more' to longer words ('kind/kinder', 'beautiful/more beautiful'). The regular superlative is formed by the addition of the suffix 'est' to shorter words and 'most' to longer words. Note, however, that some common adjectives are irregular.

Nominative The nominative is the plain form that describes a noun.	Comparative The comparative implies a comparison between the noun and something else.	Superlative The superlative is the ultimate degree of a particular quality.
Examples long small big fast bad good far	**Examples** longer smaller bigger faster worse better farther/further	**Examples** longest smallest biggest fastest worst best farthest/furthest

Adverbs

Adverbs provide extra information about the time, place or manner in which the action of a verb happened.

An **adverb** is a word that modifies a verb.

Manner Provides information about the manner in which the action was done.	Ali *quickly* ran home. The cat climbed *fearfully* up the tree.
Time Provides information about the time at which the action occurred.	*Yesterday* Ali ran home. *Sometimes* the cat climbed up the tree.
Place Provides information about where the action took place.	*Outside* Ali ran home. *In the garden* the cat climbed up the tree.

Variations in the degree of intensity of an adverb are indicated by other adjectives such as 'very', 'rather', 'quite' and 'somewhat'. Comparative forms include 'very quickly', 'rather slowly', and 'most happily'.

The majority of single-word adverbs are made by adding 'ly' to an adjective: 'quick/quickly', 'slow/slowly' and so on.

Prepositions

Prepositions show how nouns or pronouns are positioned in relation to other nouns and pronouns in the same sentence. This can often be the location of one thing in relation to another in space, such as 'on', 'over', 'near'; or time, such as 'before', 'after'.

A **preposition** is a word or phrase that shows the relationship of one thing to another.

Prepositions are usually placed before a noun. They can consist of one word (*The cat* in *the tree...*), two words (*The cat* close to *the gate...*) or three (*The cat* on top of *the roof...*).

Determiners

There are different types of determiner:

A **determiner** identifies whether a noun is known or unknown.

Articles are the most common type: 'the' (definite article) and 'a' or 'an' (indefinite article).

Possessives are often possessive pronouns such as 'my', 'your', 'our', but can also be nouns with an apostrophe, with or without an 's' (as in *Jane's car*, *the Prime Minister's speech*, *the girls' results*.)

Demonstratives are used to show the relation of the speaker to an object. There are four demonstrative pronouns in English 'this', 'that', 'these', 'those'. (See page 150.)

Quantifiers are used to express the quantity of a noun, for example: (indefinite quantity) 'some', 'many', 'several'; (definite quantity) 'every', 'both', 'all', 'four', 'seventy'.

Connectives

The job of a connective is to maintain cohesion through a piece of text.

> A **connective** is a word or phrase that links clauses or sentences.

Connectives can be:
- Conjunctions – connect clauses within one sentence.
- Connecting adverbs – connect ideas in separate sentences.

Conjunctions

Conjunctions are a special type of connective. There are two types: coordinating and subordinating.

Coordinating conjunctions connect clauses of equal weight. For example: *I like cake and I like tea.* Coordinating conjunctions include: 'and', 'but', 'or' and 'so'.

Subordinating conjunctions are used where the clauses of unequal weight, they begin a subordinate clause. For example: *The dog barked because he saw the burglar.* Subordinating conjunctions include: 'because', 'when', 'while', 'that', 'although', 'if', 'until', 'after', before' and 'since'.

Name of conjunction	Nature of conjunction	Examples
Addition	One or more clause together	We had our tea *and* went out to play.
Opposition	One or more clauses in opposition	I like coffee *but* my brother hates it. It could rain *or* it could snow.
Time	One or more clauses connected over time	Toby had his tea *then* went out to play. The bus left *before* we reached the stop.
Cause	One or more clauses causing or caused by another	I took a map *so that* we wouldn't get lost. We got lost *because* we had the wrong map.

Connecting adverbs

The table below provides the function of the adverbs and examples of the type of words used for that purpose.

Addition	'also', 'furthermore', 'moreover', 'likewise'
Opposition	'however', 'never the less', 'on the other hand'
Time	'just then', 'meanwhile', 'later'
Result	'therefore', 'as a result'
Reinforcing	'besides', 'anyway'
Explaining	'for example', 'in other words'
Listing	'first of all', 'finally'

3. Understanding sentences

Types of sentence

The four main types of sentence are declarative, interrogative, imperative and exclamatory. The function of a sentence has an effect on the word order; imperatives, for example, often begin with a verb.

Sentence type	Function	Examples
Declarative	Makes a statement	The house is down the lane. Joe rode the bike.
Interrogative	Asks a question	Where is the house? What is Joe doing?
Imperative	Issues a command or direction	Turn left at the traffic lights. Get on your bike!
Exclamatory	Issues an interjection	Wow, what a mess! Oh no!

Sentences: Clauses and complexities

Phrases

A phrase is a set of words performing a grammatical function. In the sentence *The little, old, fierce dog brutally chased the sad and fearful cat*, there are three distinct units performing grammatical functions. The first phrase in this sentence essentially names the dog and provides descriptive information. This is a noun phrase, performing the job of a noun – 'the little, old, fierce dog'. To do this the phrase uses adjectives.

The important thing to look out for is the way in which words build around a key word in a phrase. So here the words 'little', 'old' and 'fierce' are built around the word 'dog'. In examples like these, 'dog' is referred to as the **headword** and the adjectives are termed **modifiers**. Together, the modifier and headword make up the noun phrase. Modifiers can also come after the noun, as in *The little, old, fierce dog that didn't like cats brutally chased the sad and fearful cat*. In this example 'little', 'old' and 'fierce' are **premodifiers** and the phrase 'that didn't like cats' is a **postmodifier**. The noun phrase is just one of the types of phrase that can be made.

Phrase type	Examples
Noun phrase	The *little, old fierce dog* didn't like cats. She gave him *a carefully and colourfully covered book*.
Verb phrase	The dog *had been hiding* in the house. The man *climbed through* the window without a sound.
Adjectival phrase	The floor was *completely clean*. The floor was *so clean you could eat your dinner off it*.
Adverbial phrase	I finished my lunch *very slowly indeed*. *More confidently than usual*, she entered the room.
Prepositional phrase	The cat sat *at the top of* the tree. The phone rang *in the middle of* the night.

Notice that phrases can appear within phrases. A noun phrase like 'carefully and colourfully covered book' contains the adjectival phrase 'carefully and colourfully covered'. This string of words forms the adjectival phrase in which the words 'carefully' and 'colourfully' modify the adjective 'covered'. Together these words, 'carefully and colourfully covered', modify the noun 'book', creating a distinct noun phrase. This is worth noting as it shows how the boundaries between phrases can be blurred – a fact that can cause confusion unless borne in mind!

Clauses

Clauses are units of meaning included within a sentence, usually containing a verb and other elements linked to it. *The burglar ran* is a clause containing the definite article, noun and verb; *The burglar quickly ran from the little house* is also a clause that adds an adverb, preposition and adjective. The essential element in a clause is the verb. Clauses look very much like small sentences – indeed sentences can be constructed of just one clause: *The burglar hid, I like cake*.

Sentences can also be constructed out of a number of clauses linked together: *The burglar ran and I chased him because he stole my cake*. This sentence contains three clauses: 'The burglar ran', 'I chased him', 'he stole my cake'.

Clauses and phrases: the difference

Clauses include participants in an action denoted by a verb. Phrases, however, need not necessarily contain a verb. These phrases make little sense on their own: 'without a sound', 'very slowly indeed'. They work as part of a clause.

Simple, compound and complex sentences

The addition of clauses to single-clause sentences (simple sentences) can make multi-clause sentences (complex or compound sentences).

Simple sentences are made up of one clause, for example: *The dog barked, Sam was scared*.

Compound sentences are made up of clauses added to clauses. In compound sentences each of the clauses is of equal value; no clause is dependent on another. An example of a compound sentence is: *The dog barked and the parrot squawked*. Both these clauses are of equal importance: 'The dog barked', 'the parrot squawked'. Other compound sentences include, for example: *I like coffee and I like chocolate, I like coffee, but I don't like tea*.

Complex sentences are made up of a main clause with a subordinate clause or clauses. Subordinate clauses make sense in relation to the main clause. They say something about it and are dependent upon it, such as in the sentences: *The dog barked because he saw a burglar; Sam was scared so he phoned the police*.

In both these cases the subordinate clause ('he saw a burglar', 'he phoned the police') is elaborating on the main clause. They explain why the dog barked or why Sam was scared and, in doing so, are subordinate to those actions. The reader needs to see the main clauses to fully appreciate what the subordinate ones are stating.

Subject and object

The **subject** of a sentence or clause is the agent that performs the action denoted by the verb – *Shaun threw the ball*. The **object** is the agent to which the verb is done – 'ball'. It could be said that the subject does the verb to the object (a simplification but a useful one). The simplest type of sentence is known as the SVO (subject–verb–object) sentence (or clause), as in *You lost your way*, *I found the book* and *Lewis met Chloe*.

The active voice and the passive voice

These contrast two ways of saying the same thing:

Active voice	Passive voice
I found the book.	The book was found by me.
Megan met Ben.	Ben was met by Megan.
The cow jumped over the moon.	The moon was jumped over by the cow.

The two types of clause put the same subject matter in a different voice. Passive clauses are made up of a subject and verb followed by an agent.

The book	was found by	me.
subject	verb	agent
Ben	was met by	Megan.
subject	verb	agent

Sentences can be written in the active or the passive voice. A sentence can be changed from the active to the passive voice by:
- moving the subject to the end of the clause
- moving the object to the start of the clause
- changing the verb or verb phrase by placing a form of the verb 'be' before it (as in 'was found')
- changing the verb or verb phrase by placing 'by' after it.

In passive clauses the agent can be deleted, either because it does not need mentioning or because a positive choice is made to omit it. Texts on science may leave out the agent, with sentences such as *The water is added to the salt and stirred*.

4. Punctuation

Punctuation provides marks within sentences that guide the reader. Speech doesn't need punctuation (and would sound bizarre if it included noises for full stops and so on). In speech, much is communicated by pausing, changing tone and so on. In writing, the marks within and around a sentence provide indications of when to pause, when something is being quoted and so on.

Punctuation	Uses	Examples
A	**Capital letter** 1. Starts a sentence. 2. Indicates proper nouns. 3. Emphasises certain words.	1. All I want is cake. 2. You can call me Al. 3. I want it TOMORROW!
.	**Full stop** Ends sentences that are not questions or exclamations.	This is a sentence.
?	**Question mark** Ends a sentence that is a question.	Is this a question?
!	**Exclamation mark** Ends a sentence that is an exclamation.	Don't do that!
" " ' '	**Inverted commas (or quotation/speech marks)** Encloses direct speech. Can be double or single.	"Help me," the man yelled. 'Help me,' the man yelled.
,	**Comma** 1. Places a pause between clauses within a sentence. 2. Separates items in a list. 3. Separates adjectives in a series. 4. Completely encloses clauses inserted in a sentence. 5. Marks speech from words denoting who said them.	1. We were late, although it didn't matter. 2. You will need eggs, butter and flour. 3. I wore a long, green, frilly skirt. 4. We were, after we had rushed to get there, late for the film. 5. 'Thank you,' I said.
–	**Hyphen** Connects elements of certain words.	Re-read, south-west.
:	**Colon** 1. Introduces lists (including examples). 2. Introduces summaries. 3. Introduces (direct) quotations. 4. Introduces a second clause that expands or illustrates the meaning of the first.	1. To go skiing these are the main items you will need: a hat, goggles, gloves and sunscreen. 2. We have learned the following on the ski slope: do a snow plough to slow down. 3. My instructor always says: 'Bend those knees.' 4. The snow hardened: it turned into ice.

Punctuation	Uses	Examples
;	**Semicolon** 1. Separates two closely linked clauses, and shows there is a link between them. 2. Separates items in a complex list.	1. On Tuesday, the bus was late; the train was early. 2. You can go by aeroplane, train and taxi; Channel tunnel train, coach, then a short walk; or aeroplane and car.
'	**Apostrophe of possession** Denotes the ownership of one thing by another (see page 159).	This is Mona's scarf. These are the teachers' books.
'	**Apostrophe of contraction** Shows the omission of a letter(s) when two (or occasionally more) words are contracted.	Don't walk on the grass.
•••	**Ellipsis** 1. Shows the omission of words. 2. Indicates a pause.	1. The teacher moaned, 'Look at this floor… a mess… this class…' 2. Lou said: 'I think I locked the door… no, hang on, did I?'
( )	**Brackets** Contains a parenthesis – a word or phrase added to a sentence to give a bit more information.	The cupboard (which had been in my family for years) was broken.
—	**Dash** 1. Indicates additional information, with more emphasis than a comma. 2. Indicates a pause, especially for effect at the end of a sentence. 3. Contains extra information (used instead of brackets).	1. She is a teacher – and a very good one too. 2. We all know what to expect – the worst. 3. You finished that job – and I don't know how – before the deadline.

Adding an apostrophe of possession

The addition of an apostrophe can create confusion. The main thing to look at is the noun
– ask:

- Is it singular or plural?
- Does it end in an 's'?

If the noun is singular and doesn't end in 's', you add an apostrophe and an 's', for example: *Indra's house* *the firefighter's bravery*	If the noun is singular and ends in 's', you add an apostrophe and an 's', for example: *the bus's wheels* *Thomas's pen*
If the noun is plural and doesn't end in 's', you add an apostrophe and an 's', for example: *the women's magazine* *the geese's flight*	If the noun is plural and ends in 's', you add an apostrophe but don't add an 's', for example: *the boys' clothes* *the dancers' performance*